# FIRST WORDS **TO NEW CHRISTIANS**

## Register This New Book

### Benefits of Registering*

- ✓ FREE **replacements** of lost or damaged books
- ✓ FREE **audiobook** – *Pilgrim's Progress*, audiobook edition
- ✓ FREE information about new titles and other **freebies**

www.anekopress.com/new-book-registration

*See our website for requirements and limitations.

# FIRST WORDS **TO NEW CHRISTIANS**

**HOW TO RUN WITH ENDURANCE THE RACE SET BEFORE YOU**

**ROBERT BOYD**

aNEKO
PRESS

We love hearing from our readers. Please contact us at www.anekopress.com/questions-comments with any questions, comments, or suggestions.

*First Words to Young Christians*
© 2020 by Aneko Press
All rights reserved. First edition 1905
Revised edition 2020

No part of this book may be reproduced, stored in a retrieval system, or transmitted in any form or by any means – electronic, mechanical, photocopying, recording, or otherwise, without written permission from the publisher.

Unless otherwise indicated, scripture quotations are taken from the New American Standard Bible® (NASB), copyright © 1960, 1962, 1963, 1968, 1971, 1972, 1973, 1975, 1977, 1995 by The Lockman Foundation. Used by permission. www.Lockman.org.

Scripture quotations marked KJV are from The Authorized (King James) Version. Rights in the Authorized Version in the United Kingdom are vested in the Crown. Reproduced by permission of the Crown's patentee, Cambridge University Press.

*Cover Design: Jonathan Lewis*
*Editors: Paul Miller and Ruth Clark*

Printed in the United States of America
Aneko Press
www.anekopress.com
Aneko Press, Life Sentence Publishing, and our logos are trademarks of
Life Sentence Publishing, Inc.
203 E. Birch Street
P.O. Box 652
Abbotsford, WI 54405

**RELIGION / Christian Living / Spiritual Growth**

Paperback ISBN: 978-1-62245-531-7
eBook ISBN: 978-1-62245-532-4

10 9 8 7 6 5 4 3 2 1

Available where books are sold

# Contents

*Introduction* ......................................................................... ix

**Ch. 1:** Starting Right ........................................................ 1

**Ch. 2:** A Public Profession of Faith ................................ 9

**Ch. 3:** Spiritual Growth .................................................. 21

**Ch. 4:** Duties in the Church .......................................... 29

**Ch. 5:** Duties to the Pastor ............................................ 43

**Ch. 6:** Duties in Sunday School .................................... 59

**Ch. 7:** Duties in the World ............................................ 69

**Ch. 8:** Enemies of Grace ................................................ 79

**Ch. 9:** Helps and Hindrances in Daily Life .................. 89

**Ch. 10:** The Spiritual Mind ........................................... 103

**Ch. 11:** Hindrances and Helps to Spiritual-Mindedness 117

**Ch. 12:** Consecration ...................................................... 129

**Ch. 13:** How to Make a Success of the Christian Life ..... 143

**Appx. A:** How to Use the Bible .................................... 153

**Appx. B:** Tips for True Christian Living .................... 155

*Robert Boyd – A Brief Biography* ................................... 157

*Other Similar Titles* ........................................................ 163

# Introduction

I have recently often been asked by young converts where to get a book in which they might find advice that would be helpful to them. I felt the need of some good advice when I first became a Christian, and I know the value of words fitly spoken. *Like apples of gold in settings of silver is a word spoken in right circumstances* (Proverbs 25:11).

Some weeks ago a copy of this book was sent to me, and it seemed to be just the thing needed at this time. I have known the author, Dr. Boyd, for many years. I have read his work carefully, and I recommend it to all young Christians for prayerful meditation.

Dwight L. Moody

# Chapter 1

# Starting Right

I take it for granted that you have really been converted, that you depend upon nothing and no one else for salvation, but you now rest peacefully upon the atoning work of Christ. I do not ask *how* this great change has been brought about, nor what has been the specific means that the Holy Spirit has blessed to bring you to Jesus. Whether you have passed through a long process of convictions and of alternate fears and hopes, or whether, like most of the conversions mentioned in the New Testament, you were suddenly brought to submit yourself to Christ's method of salvation, is not the main issue now. You are now *in* Christ, and that is the really vital point. The great matter upon which two eternities turn and upon which life and death, heaven and hell depend – your personal faith in Christ – is now settled, and well settled; and I thank God on your behalf.

Dear reader, I congratulate you on the high honor

and the lofty distinction to which the mighty grace of God has lifted you. The greatest gift that God can bestow upon anyone is Himself. You are now an heir of God (Romans 8:17). You are able to say with holy boldness, *My beloved is mine, and I am his* (Song of Solomon 2:16). The apostle John said to the converts of his day, *Beloved, now we are children of God* (1 John 3:2), and we can rest assured that the unchanging Savior has not diminished the honors and privileges of His people since that time.

Once you are in Christ by a living faith, the whole fullness of God is yours. Your feelings and frame of mind mean nothing without Christ. Your ceremonies, beliefs, creeds, ordinances, and religious activities are all nothing without Christ, but with trust in Him, there is not any height of glory and honor in the whole universe that can be attained to which you may not ascend. If you have faith in Jesus, then you are a new creation – a new person. If you are a new creation, then you are a child of God. If you are a child of God, then you are an heir of God, and a joint-heir with Christ. *The Spirit Himself testifies with our spirit that we are children of God, and if children, heirs also, heirs of God and fellow heirs with Christ* (Romans 8:16-17). Thus united to Jesus, your inheritance is sure, for He is now in full possession of it.

You see, then, what a great thing it is to be a Christian. Indeed, it will take all eternity to unfold to us the greatness of the privilege. For now, we can only wander around the edge of the boundless subject and exclaim, *It has not appeared as yet what we will be* (1 John 3:2). As Rowland Hill once said when trying to illustrate God's love to His people, "I am unable to reach the lofty theme! Yet I do not think that the smallest fish that swims in the boundless ocean ever complains of the immeasurable vastness of the deep. So it is with me: I can plunge, with my puny capacity, into a subject, the immensity of which I shall never be able fully to comprehend."[1]

For a child of wrath, a slave of Satan, a condemned criminal, and an heir of hell to be raised to a height of privilege and glory which even angels do not attain is most wonderful to the thoughtful mind! It is a miracle of grace that you who, but a little while ago, were full of enmity against God with your heart set on evil and your footsteps hastening down the broad road to destruction, should now be what you are and where you are.

No wonder the angels rejoiced over you in that happy hour when you turned to Christ! *There is joy in the presence of the angels of God over one sinner who repents* (Luke 15:10). No wonder that the friends who had so long prayed and longed for your conversion rejoiced over you with such a sincere gladness! No wonder that you yourself rejoiced *with joy inexpressible and full of glory* (1 Peter 1:8).

---

[1] Rowland Hill (1744-1833) was an English evangelical preacher. This quote is found in *The Life of the Rev. Rowland Hill, A. M* by Edwin Stoney.

## Now what?

Now that you are a Christian, it becomes a most important question: What *kind* of a Christian are you going to be? Are you going to be one modeled after people's opinions, or will you follow after the Bible standard? Are you a *Christian*, as defined by scripture?

People have a way of trying to avoid the point of divine truth on this subject from their consciences by saying, "Christians *ought* to do so and so"; but the Word of God does not speak in this way. It does not say that Christians *ought* to be the light of the world, but that they *are* so (Matthew 5:14). It does not say that they *ought* to be holy, but that they *are* possessed of that character (1 Peter 2:9). It is not merely that they *ought* to be bold and faithful witnesses for Christ in this dark and sinful world, but that they really *are* so testifying (2 Corinthians 3:2-3).

This is a solemn passage: *For no man can lay a foundation other than the one which is laid, which is Jesus Christ. Now if any man builds on the foundation with gold, silver, precious stones, wood, hay, straw, their work will be shown for what it is, because the Day will bring it to light. It will be revealed with fire, and the fire will test the quality of each person's work* (1 Corinthians 3:11-13).

This is a good foundation, a most precious foundation, the best that only God could lay, firm and secure as His eternal throne – but what are you going to build upon it? Will it be the wood, hay, and stubble of worldly-mindedness, carnal affections, sinful tempers, and low, narrow, and selfish views? Or will it be the gold, silver, and precious stones of holiness, self-denial, heavenly affections, and earnest love to God and others, showing itself in works of faith and in labors of love? Depend upon it that day by day and little by little you are building up some kind of character, and you need to see to it that it is such as will honor the glorious foundation, and such as the fires of judgment will not have to burn up.

The temple of a holy life, built upon the foundation laid in Zion, greatly honors God and commands the admiration of even worldly and wicked people. The following true story, told to me by someone familiar with all the circumstances, will illustrate this:

In one of the older states lived a heathen, the owner of a sawmill that was situated by the side of the highway over which a large portion of a Christian congregation passed every Sunday to and from the church. This unsaved man, having no regard for the Lord's Day, was just as busy, and his mill was just as noisy, on that holy day as on any other.

Before long it was observed, however, that at a certain time before the church service, the mill would stop, remain silent, and appear to be deserted for a few moments. Then its noise and clatter would start up again and continue until about the close of the service, when for a short time it again ceased.

It was soon noticed that one specific deacon of the church passed the mill to the place of worship during the silent interval, and so punctual was he to the hour that the infidel knew when to stop the mill so that it would be silent when the deacon was passing, although he paid no regard when others passed by. On being asked why he paid this mark of respect to the deacon, he replied, "The deacon professes just what the rest of you do, but he also *lives* such a life that it makes me feel bad *here* (putting his hand upon his heart) to run my mill while he is passing by."

There are large numbers of individuals who, after their professed conversion, drop out of sight, and you would never know that they were Christians unless they told you so, or you learned that they were members of a church. It is true that every Christian cannot occupy a prominent and leading position in the work of Christ's kingdom, but everyone can be a worker for Jesus. Everyone can boldly unfurl his colors and let it be known whose side he is on.

Resolve in your heart that you will be a *laborer*, not a *loiterer*, in the Lord's vineyard. Resolve that whether your life is a long one, or very short, as people use the term, it will be filled with Christian activity.

A life is not to be numbered by years, but by what a person has done for God. McCheyne, Summerfield, Nott, and Dudley Tyng all died young, and yet they were old in fruits unto holiness – their life's work done and well done![2] Let yours, like theirs, be a life in earnest,

---

2 **Robert Murray McCheyne** (1813-1843) was a Scottish preacher known for love and holiness and for developing a widely used plan to read through the Bible in a year.
**John Summerfield** (1798-1825) was a Methodist evangelist and preacher in America. A newspaper wrote of him that when he preached, "he appears as if the very breathings of the Spirit were on him and his countenance is lighted with a fire bright and holy." He died at the age of twenty-seven, a month after helping to found the American Bible Society.
**Abner Kingman Nott** (1834-1859) was a Baptist pastor in New York City. His memoir was written by his brother.

a life that shows not Christianity as one thing among other things in your life, but as absolutely *everything*! Let yours be a consecrated life in spirit, soul, and body. Let your time, talents, and property be all wholly dedicated to God.

## Warning

Let me warn you of one thing: as you have begun by finding peace in Christ, continue to seek it in Him. Many young converts make great mistakes here. At first their feelings and affections have been warm and exuberant. In the fire and fervency of their first love they feel as if they could sing about Jesus all day long. However, when these glowing feelings, from whatever cause, begin to decline, they sink into despondency and feel as if they have lost Christ. Attitudes and feelings change with the state of our health, the state of the weather, the circumstances in which we are placed, and through a great variety of moral and physical causes – but Jesus Christ never changes! He is the same yesterday, today, and forever.

> Jesus Christ never changes!

We have known some people who never thought they had any enjoyment of Christianity unless they

---

**Dudley Tyng** (1825-1858) was an Episcopal pastor in Philadelphia known for his direct preaching and opposition to slavery. As he was dying, he told his father, "Stand up for Jesus, father, and tell my brethren of the ministry to stand up for Jesus." Pastor George Duffield was moved by the funeral, and he wrote a poem that he read the next week during his sermon. This poem has become a well-known hymn, "Stand Up, Stand Up for Jesus."

were experiencing much emotion. The meeting that did not melt them into tears or lift them up to the heights of ecstatic rapture was not a good meeting. The calm statement of divine truth, the earnest study of the Bible to know the will of God, and the prayerfulness and self-examination when one is alone with God all appear to such people to be dull and uninteresting. They are like habitual readers of fictional romance novels; they have no interest in what is solid and instructive. My dear reader, avoid this at the very beginning of your Christian career, and let Jesus, who alone is the Author, be also the Finisher of your faith.

> *Fixing our eyes on Jesus, the author and perfecter of faith* (Hebrews 12:2).

# Chapter 2

# A Public Profession of Faith

There is not a nobler sight in the world than to see someone commit himself unreservedly to the best of causes – the cause of Christ. It is a noble sight to see someone who is determined to stand by the cause of Christ at all hazards – to live for it, to work for it, to suffer for it, and (if need be) to die for it, but never to forsake it. Such a sight is morally sublime, and it challenges the admiration of all who are capable of appreciating moral beauty. David said, *I shall pay my vows to the LORD, oh may it be in the presence of all His people* (Psalm 116:14).

As soon as a person is converted, it becomes his imperative duty to make a public profession of loyalty to the Lord Jesus. Some churches are in the habit of keeping young converts back from a public profession of their intent to follow Jesus for a time in order to prove their sincerity and their steadfastness. As a pastor, I used to encourage this practice in some cases, and I now regret it. It does not have even a shadow of support in the Word of God.

When Christ sent forth His disciples, clothed with His high commission to preach the gospel and to establish churches, the promised Holy Spirit accompanied the word spoken by them, and in some cases, thousands were converted, and on the same day – often in the same hour – they were baptized and added to the church. To put a tender little lamb out on a snowbank exposed to the bleak winds in order to see whether it will live is entirely a modern invention.

The early churches were never guilty of such foolishness. They required a profession of conversion, repentance toward God, and faith in the Lord Jesus. Where these were given and when there was nothing in the life of the candidate to contradict the profession, they were at once baptized and added to the church.

It is true that they were sometimes deceived and they sometimes admitted unworthy persons, just as churches are deceived now, but that is due to the imperfection of human nature, and it is an evil that no amount of delay in the reception of members will either reduce or prevent. It is your duty as a Christian to offer yourself at once to the service of Christ, and if anyone throws any delay in your way, the responsibility is theirs, not yours.

## Meeting with the body of Christ

But you may say, "Can I not be as good a Christian without being united with other Christians as with being with other Christians?" To this I can give a most decided answer in the negative. No, you cannot. Indeed, the question itself is absurd. It is equivalent to asking, "Can I not be as good a Christian without obeying Christ as with obeying Him?" Christ established His church upon earth. He purchased her with His own blood. He laid the foundation upon which He has built with His own bleeding hands. He has appointed her ordinances and her government. He established her officers and gave them their gifts and qualifications for her special edification. He has watched over her in all ages and has pledged His princely word that *the gates of Hades will not overpower it* (Matthew 16:18). Do you think that it can now be agreeable to the Savior's will to see His church neglected by His professed followers? No. To live outside of the community of local believers in Christ is to live in sin, in constant disobedience, and this must bring condemnation and darkness upon the mind.

> Christ established His church upon earth.

To be with other Christians in seeking and serving God and helping and encouraging others is the Christian's home while upon earth. It is there that he is supported and comforted and prepared for the society of the just made perfect, the church of the firstborn, written in heaven (Hebrews 12:23). Though Jesus, the Head of the church, is perfect, her members are not. They have their imperfections and sinful tempers. Irritations and contentions sometimes mar her holy beauty; but her most pious members can say, "O Zion, with all thy faults I love thee still!"[3]

> Beyond my highest joy,
> > I prize her heavenly ways,
> Her sweet communion, solemn vows,
> > Her hymns of love and praise.
>
> For her my tears shall fall,
> > For her my prayers ascend;
> To her my cares and toils be given,
> > Till toils and cares shall end.[4]

For those who try to live as Christians without uniting with other true Christians, there is another consideration worthy of attention. If it is right for you to remain out of the church, it is right for someone else to do it; and if it is right for two to do it, it would be right for two thousand, or for all Christians to do it. Thus, on the principle mentioned, there would be no gatherings of Christians, no ministers of the gospel, no bond of union to bind Christians together, and no organization by which the body of the faithful could work together for the overthrow of evil and the establishment of good in the world.

Would this be a desirable state of things? You think that it would not, and yet, as far as your influence goes on this point, it leads to just such results. Our Lord says,

---

[3] This is likely a reference from William Cowper's poem "The Task," in which he writes, "England, with all thy faults, I love thee still."

[4] These are two stanzas from Timothy Dwight's hymn, "I Love Thy Kingdom, Lord."

*He who is not with Me is against Me* (Matthew 12:30), and the same is true concerning His church. If you are not with it, you must be against it, at least to a certain extent. The world will point to you as one who has something against the church, or else you would have joined with her. The better your character and reputation are, the greater damage your standing alone will do. The scoffers will say that you are too good a person to have anything to do with such people. They will count you as being on their side.

## Unworthy?

There are some young converts who are kept back by conscientious, though mistaken, views in regard to themselves. Someone might say, "I feel utterly unworthy to be part of the body of Christ." Now this self-distrust is a good thing when kept in its proper place. True faith in Jesus always has a lack of self-trust connected with it, for before we can depend entirely on Him, we must be emptied of self.

It has been compared to a young tree. The trunk grows upward from the little seed, and the root grows downward from the same seed, growing and springing in different directions from the same source. In the same way, the same seed of faith in Christ springs upward in confidence toward God, and downward in distrust in ourselves. However, if this distrust is used to lead us to neglect Christ's plain commands, it is being corrupted for a wrongful purpose. It is turning the grace of God into sin.

Jesus does not ask you to make a public profession of your faith because you are worthy. It was not because you were worthy that He pardoned your sins and shed His love abroad in your heart (Romans 5:5), and He asks you now to show your love to Him by keeping His commands and doing those things that will be pleasing in His sight – from a principle of simply doing what is right.

## False humility

There are others who say, "I am afraid to make a public profession in case I fall away into sin and dishonor it." This sounds very humble, but it really springs from pride of heart. It goes upon the principle that you are to be your own support and to stand without divine support. Did God make you a Christian, or did you make yourself one? If He made you a Christian, do you not think that He is able to keep you one? *You of little faith, why did you doubt?* (Matthew 14:31). He who gives you the strength to do one duty can support you as you carry out another. Go on boldly, and in the path of right you have nothing to fear. The Master you serve will surround you with invisible armor so that none can harm you. The promises of God will stand up around you like the mountains around Jerusalem. *As the mountains surround Jerusalem, so the LORD surrounds His people from this time forth and forever* (Psalm 125:2).

## A PUBLIC PROFESSION OF FAITH

This reminds me of an incident that occurred on board a British ship at the battle of the Nile. There was only one Bible among seven hundred men. This Bible belonged to a pious sailor who did not forget to let his light shine before others (Matthew 5:16). He read to others from his Bible, and by doing so, a little praying circle was formed, numbering thirteen in all.

Just before the battle, they all met and commended themselves to God in prayer, expecting never again to meet in this world. Their ship was in the thickest of the storm, and all around them their comrades fell, never to rise again. At one gun, where two of the men were stationed, three other soldiers were killed by one cannonball, but there they stood firm to their posts, clad in an armor invisible to mortal eyes, but more impenetrable than steel. When the battle was over, those who were left had agreed to meet, if possible. What joy they had to find all thirteen men assembled, not one of them even wounded! What a thanksgiving meeting that must have been!

The same God who preserved those men from physical danger can keep you from all moral danger, so that in the fiercest temptations, when the fiery darts of the Enemy fall thick around you, the divine shield will defend you, and you will stand steadfast and unmovable. *Therefore, my beloved brethren, be steadfast, immovable, always abounding in the work of the Lord, knowing that your toil is not in vain in the Lord* (1 Corinthians 15:58).

## Fear and shame

Sometimes people are kept back from making a public profession of their faith by the fear of man. They fear the displeasure of their unsaved relatives or the ridicule of their former coworkers or friends. They also dread publicly testifying to what Christ has done for their souls – even among fellow Christians.

This is very unworthy of those for whose salvation the blessed Savior *endured the cross, despising the shame* (Hebrews 12:2). That gracious Friend tells us, *If anyone wishes to come after Me, he must deny himself, and take up his cross daily and follow Me* (Luke 9:23). We must often sacrifice the lesser things so that we may enjoy the greater. We must often pass by the favor of people and the smiles of the world in order to have the favor of God and the happiness of a good conscience.

These are the plain and searching principles that Jesus lays down, and we can see that they are highly reasonable and proper. If any try to avoid these principles, it must be because they prefer the favor of people to that of God, or because they are ashamed of the Lord Jesus. *For whoever is ashamed of Me and My words, the Son of Man will be ashamed of him when He comes in His glory, and the glory of the Father and of the holy angels* (Luke 9:26).

You must come out from this hesitating, compromising spirit or you can never be a happy and useful Christian. Your mind will be tossed to and fro by conflicting influences, and you will wander about, wrapped up in a dark and gloomy haze of doubt and uncertainty. Suppose that when Paul was converted he had tried to keep it all to himself in order to avoid persecution. What would his Christianity have amounted to? Or what if Luther, when he discovered in his Bible the doctrine of justification by faith, had kept it all in his own heart and in his cell so that he would not get involved in some trouble and controversy? Would God ever have honored him as He did? No. The principle that God acts on in such matters is, *Those who honor me I will honor* (1 Samuel 2:30).

## Which group?

Perhaps you are not sure which group of Christians to be with. This is a matter of importance, and it demands the prayerful and careful study of the Word of God. You should not join a church because your friends and companions are going to join it or have already done so. It is not a good reason to join a church because you think you would feel more at home there. It should not be a matter of mere feeling, but of intelligent principle. The Bible is the only standard of appeal in all matters of faith and practice, and after an honest and faithful examination of that holy Book, you should join with that body of Christians whom you conscientiously believe to be nearest to the Word of God.

I believe that the church to which I belong comes nearer to the faith and practice of the church established by Christ and His apostles than any other that I know of. If I did not so believe, it would be my duty to leave it. If I knew of any other nearer to the Bible, it would be my duty to join it. Every intelligent and conscientious Christian, it is to be presumed, acts on the same principle. A false liberality would no doubt call this bigotry, but those who have learned to *contend earnestly for the faith which was once for all handed down to the saints* (Jude v. 3) are not easily frightened by big, intense, pretentious words. On this matter let the Word of God be your only guide.

Though I do not feel at liberty to counsel you as to which specific group of Christians to join with, I do most earnestly urge you to place yourself under a faithful and evangelical ministry. Do not attend the ministry of any man who does not preach Christ in the fullest sense of the word. Christ may be in his creed, but if He is not in his sermons, your soul will starve under him.

Charles Spurgeon tells us that when he was spiritually awakened, he wandered from church to church to find out how he could be saved, but he never heard the gospel. One minister preached the experience of the people of God, and he felt that he had nothing to do with that. Another told him of the blessedness of the regenerated, but he did not think that applied to him. On one Sunday the text would be, *Do not be deceived, God is not mocked* (Galatians 6:7). On another it would be, *The wages of sin is death* (Romans 6:23).

Spurgeon tells us that he became worse and worse after hearing sermons that nearly drove him to despair. Then there would be texts for good people, but not a word for him. At last he accidently heard a very humble preacher, and his text was, *Turn to Me and be saved, all the ends of the earth* (Isaiah 45:22). That was what he needed to hear. He felt that it was intended for him.

"Look, look to Jesus," said the preacher, "and you will be saved this moment – you will be lightened of your burden!" Spurgeon tells us that he did then and there look to Jesus by faith, and he felt as if he could have sprung into the air, for his burden of sin was gone!

> Place yourself under the instruction of one who will delight frequently to lead you near the cross.

A pastor may preach ably and eloquently. He may be a good man and may preach a great deal of valuable truth. He may even preach a great deal *about* Christ, and yet not preach Christ in the scriptural sense of the term. Place yourself under the instruction of one who will delight frequently to lead you near the cross.

> Oppressed with noon-day's scorching heat,
>     To yonder cross I flee;
> Beneath its shelter take my seat;
>     No shade like this for me!
>
> Beneath that cross clear waters burst,
>     A fountain sparkling free;
> And there I quench my desert thirst;
>     No spring like this for me!
>
> For burdened ones a resting place,
>     Beside that cross I see;
> Here I cast off my weariness;
>     No rest like this for me!
>
> —Horatius Bonar, "The Shadow of the Cross"

# Chapter 3

# Spiritual Growth

Much is said today about human progress. Poetry and eloquence have taken their loftiest flights in praise of it. Ours has so often been called a progressive age that with all our vanity we are beginning to tire of the endless repetition. Progress is undoubtedly a good thing, if it is of the right kind. Many people think that they are making progress by rejecting what is old and eagerly adopting what is new.

Change is one thing, but true progress is another. All true progress, that which is pleasing to God, must come from within, not from without. The eagle might have wings tied to it, but it could never make any progress with them, for it must have wings that grow up out of its own body with which to soar up from its favorite peak on the sky-piercing mountain. All true human progress must begin in the heart, and it must be put there by His hand who plants the glorious galaxy of stars upon the dark brow of night.

We all know that the body, under the influence of proper food, air, and exercise, is capable of growth in strength and in the development of all its powers. The same law of growth holds good in regard to the eternal soul. That was a remarkable wish of the apostle John for his beloved friend Gaius: *I pray that in all respects you may prosper and be in good health, just as your soul prospers* (3 John v. 2). Sadly, if the degree of our physical health were to be regulated by the health of the soul, what a nation of invalids we would be! How many there are who are sensitively alive to the needs of their bodies, but utterly neglectful of the immortal soul lodged within! Many a large, sturdy, vigorous body covers a poor, weak, sickly, starved soul, so that the disproportion between the soul and its outward covering is as great as it would be if a very small boy were clothed in his father's clothes.

## Life in Christ

There can be no growth without life. Dead things do not grow, but decay. You could decorate a dead tree to any extent. You could paint and varnish over the dead, rotten trunk, but unless you could put life into it, there could be no growth. Despite all your decorations, the process of decay would go on, and one dead limb after another would fall down, fit only for the fire. In the same way, there can be no spiritual growth unless we are connected with Jesus by a living faith. He says, *I AM the resurrection and the life* (John 11:25).

For the branch to get life and strength from the vine,

it must be *in* the vine, and not merely *near* it. Even if it were tied to the vine, it would get no strength and bear no fruit, but would simply hang there as an unsightly object, rustling in the wind. Even so, one may be connected with a church by an outward profession and may remain so connected for many years, but if there is not a union with Christ, there can be no spiritual growth and no bringing forth of fruit unto holiness.

The Ottawa River in Canada rises to a great height at certain seasons of the year, and then suddenly falls again, leaving logs on the high banks and dead branches and other rubbish hanging in the tops of the trees. There they lie, useless things, rotting in the sun and rain that are making other things grow. I have often looked sadly upon them, thinking how much they are like those Christless professors of religion, who in some wild flood of excitement have been swept into the church, and when the excitement has gone down, are left there with no spiritual life!

They may be moral and nice and never do any outward act of public sin for which they can be cast out of the church, but they are spiritually dead. They might hold solid doctrinal beliefs. They might sing and pray and go through religious duties with mechanical regularity, but since there is no Christ in their religion, there is no life. Sometimes, on important occasions, they might put on a show of life, just as a corpse may by muscle contractions stimulated by an electrical current (galvanism) be made to roll its eyes and wildly toss its lifeless limbs – but it is only a spasmodic exertion that soon settles down into the stillness and corruption of death. How sad it is to look upon these moral imitations, these types of the old Pharisee, and to think how few of them are ever likely to be saved! O that the divine Spirit might give power to the appeal, *Awake, sleeper, and arise from the dead, and Christ will shine on you* (Ephesians 5:14).

## Growing life

Where there is true union with Christ, there will not only be life, but there will also be growing life: *I came that they may have life, and have it abundantly* (John 10:10). However, our eyes must be fixed only upon Christ, and our whole hope must be centered in Him. He alone must be our strength. We must not be looking partly at ourselves and partly at Christ, now glancing at our own feelings as a ground of hope, and then at His merits.

It is a common thing for young converts to make great mistakes here. Deeply conscientious, they dread deceiving themselves, and being fervently desirous to grow in grace, they watch and analyze every emotion of their minds. In the meantime, while focusing on these things, their attention is turned away from Jesus, the great source of all spiritual life and growth, and so they find themselves plunged into a dark jungle of doubts and fears.

We have seen children, in their great concern for the growth of their little gardens, keep pulling up their plants every now and again to see if they are growing. The farmer who would pull up his corn to measure if it was growing would not have much of a crop in the fall. The Christian who turns away his eyes from the Savior to analyze his own experience and who is constantly examining his every motive and feeling to try to make it say something good concerning himself will find that instead of growth and strength, leanness has come into his soul.

If you constantly remain near to Christ, taking Him as your only hope and His spotless life as your clear example, spiritual progress will be seen in your life, brighter and brighter to the perfect day. With knowledge in your mind, grace in your heart, and obedience in your life, there will be a symmetry of character that will lead others to glorify your Father in heaven. In the difficult conflict with your besetting sins, Christ will be your strength. He will stay with you until your last foe lies vanquished on the field. Hasty and impulsive passions will be displaced by calm and holy rest in God. Unholy bursts of forceful temper will be subdued by the meekness of Jesus. Irritability and impatience will give way to holy submission to God's will. Worldly-mindedness will be overcome by communion with God and a clearer conception of the grandeur and glory of eternal things.

## Growth is gradual

Remember that all growth is gradual. You do not become a great and holy man or woman in an hour, or in some moment of strong religious excitement, or because you have a godly friend. On such occasions, the soul may receive a heavenly stimulus that will greatly increase its strength, but its real growth will be a progressive work, day by day.

In the morning, let the thought fill your mind: "My life is made up of days, and as the main business of life is to live to the glory of God, how can I best glorify Him today?" Seek earnestly to live to God for that one day, as if it were your last. However urgent your duties may be, be sure that you make time for two things: speaking to God, and hearing God speak to you. By speaking to God, I mean prayer, and by hearing God speak to you, I mean reading the Bible. It is said of Colonel Gardiner that when in his battle campaigns he had to march before daybreak, he always made a point of rising early enough to have time for prayer and reading the Scriptures.

Instead of making your Christianity bend to your worldly convenience, make your worldly convenience bend to your Christianity. Pray earnestly and believingly for growth in grace and for strength to support you amid the trials and temptations of life, but do not put prayer in the place of duties that you ought to do yourself. God says you are to watch as well as pray. If you pray that God would give you the victory over some besetting sin, but you neglect to watch against that sin and you fail to cut off every temptation to its indulgence as far as you can, you cannot expect God to answer your prayer.

God will do nothing for us that we can do for

ourselves. Prayer is not intended to encourage laziness. When we pray for deliverance from evil and victory over our sins, we must watch, fight, and struggle against them, or else our prayer is only a solemn mockery. God brought it as a very heavy charge against Israel that *their deeds will not allow them to return to their God* (Hosea 5:4). We must be coworkers with God in the great work of growing in grace. We must shun the appearance of evil, and not even *seem* to come short. *Abstain from every form of evil* (1 Thessalonians 5:22).

It is of vital importance that we have daily communion with God through His Word. This is to be our daily bread – bread for the soul. *Man shall not live on bread alone, but by every word of God* (Luke 4:4). You would not expect a child to grow physically unless he regularly ate nourishing food, and a child of God cannot grow in grace unless he lives upon the food that God has provided.

Therefore, read a portion of the Scriptures every morning before going out into the bustle of the world. Our Lord's prayer was, *Sanctify them in the truth; Your word is truth* (John 17:17). If, then, you are to be sanctified in soul, it must be through the truths of the Word of God. Therefore, let your mind be deeply permeated with them. It is a condition of your nature that you will grow in something; if it is not in good, it will be in evil. There can be no standing still with an immortal soul. The soul craves for food, and if it is not fed and nourished by the pure words of God, it will take to itself vile and worldly husks!

## Grow

Resolve to press forward to higher attainments in the divine life. Do not be content with a low standard of piety – with merely being safe. Your example is a very high one – the Lord Jesus. Keep your eyes fixed upon Him until you are transformed into His image. An eloquent writer says:

The growth in grace is the only one not subject to decay and death. It has a vast assimilative power which nothing can resist. It feeds, therefore, on all the elements of man's life, on all the chequered experiences of his days. It feeds on joy; it feeds on sorrow. It rises by nature's growths, but does not sink in nature's decays. The outward man may perish, but the inward man is renewed day by day. Days of sorest sickness fill the springs of immortal health; and the day of death in the vocabulary of grace is but the earthly name for the first day of eternal life. Grow, then, in that which must forever grow – in that which will always be grace, although it will soon be glory, and always fresh and living as the beauty of the Saviour, or as the thoughts and affections of God.[5]

> My hopes are passing upward, onward,
>     And with my hopes my heart has gone;
> My eye is turning skyward, sunward,
>     Where glory brightens round yon throne![6]

---

5    From the sermon "Growing in Grace" by Alexander Raleigh (1817-1880), in his book, *Quiet Resting Places and Other Sermons*.

6    From "A Stranger Here" by Horatius Bonar (1808-1889).

## Chapter 4

# Duties in the Church

I take it for granted that you are now a member of Christ's church and that you have had the happy privilege to sit down at the table of the Lord. Your first time at the Lord's Table, or Communion, is a time never to be forgotten by the Christian. Of course, you are not to attach any saving efficacy or superstitious importance to that ordinance above others, but from its very nature it brings your blessed Savior directly before you, saying, *Do this in remembrance of Me* (1 Corinthians 11:24). It was instituted by the Lord's direct command and for the express purpose of commemorating His dying love, and it is to be promptly and faithfully observed until He comes in His glory.

### Faith, not feelings

Christians sometimes stay away from the Lord's Supper because their feelings are not as stirring as they would wish, or because there is some gloominess upon their minds. I hope this will never be your case. It is making our own feelings the rule of duty, instead of the positive command of Christ. It is setting up our own ideas as the standard of what we should do and what we should not do, instead of the certain and direct will of the great Head of the church. The same rule, carried out, would lead us to neglect prayer, the reading of the Bible, attendance upon the means of grace, and, basically, everything that we did not feel happy in doing at the time.

Why should Christians stay away from the very means that Jesus has instituted for their spiritual profit merely because of how they feel? It is as absurd as staying away from the fire because you are cold, or from the table because you are hungry, or refusing to take medicine because you are sick. In the keeping of God's commands there is great reward, and in waiting upon God, in the means of His appointment, the obedient soul renews its strength.[7]

> *The law of the LORD is perfect, restoring the soul; The testimony of the LORD is sure, making wise the simple. The precepts of the LORD are right, rejoicing the heart;*

---

[7] Publisher's Note: Living in persistent, open sin would be one scriptural reason to *not* partake in communion. This is, of course, different than not partaking in communion merely because of how one feels. *Therefore whoever eats the bread or drinks the cup of the Lord in an unworthy manner, shall be guilty of the body and the blood of the Lord. But a man must examine himself, and in so doing he is to eat of the bread and drink of the cup. For he who eats and drinks, eats and drinks judgment to himself if he does not judge the body rightly.* – 1 Corinthians 11:27-29

## DUTIES IN THE CHURCH

*The commandment of the LORD is pure, enlightening the eyes. The fear of the LORD is clean, enduring forever; The judgments of the LORD are true; they are righteous altogether. They are more desirable than gold, yes, than much fine gold; Sweeter also than honey and the drippings of the honeycomb. Moreover, by them Your servant is warned; In keeping them there is great reward.*
(Psalm 19:7-11)

*Those who wait for the LORD will gain new strength; They will mount up with wings like eagles, they will run and not get tired, they will walk and not become weary.*
(Isaiah 40:31)

## A good excuse?

There are others who stay away from Communion because they are offended with some of their brethren. When you turn your back on the Lord's Supper and refuse to commemorate what your Savior did for you on Calvary, you should remember that one of these days He is going to ask you for your reasons for doing so. He will not be satisfied with *excuses*, but He must have *reasons*.

Will it be a *reason* to say that you did wrong because someone else did wrong, that you deliberately concluded that you would neglect one plain duty because someone else neglected another duty? If that brother has done some great evil in the sight of God, will it mend the matter for you to do another wrong by despising Christ's ordinances?

You say that a certain brother has offended you, and so you will not come to the Communion table while he is there. Has Christ offended you also? If not, why do you seek to revenge the wrong upon your Lord and His ordinance? He urges you to come to His table in remembrance of Him, and you reply, "Lord, I will not remember You because this brother has done wrong."

Such conduct is sinful and unreasonable. It is sometimes the result of ignorance, but for the most part it is the indulgence of a bad attitude under the pretense of being conscientious. It is like Jonah, who professed to be angry on principle, and had the presumption to tell God to His face, *I do well to be angry* (Jonah 4:9).

In vindication of such conduct, this passage is often quoted: *Therefore if you are presenting your offering at the altar, and there remember that your brother has something against* you, *leave your offering there before the altar and go; first be reconciled to your brother, and then come and present your offering* (Matthew 5:23-24).

This has no special reference to the Lord's Supper, and if it had, it would be no excuse for the conduct we are condemning. It says, *If you . . . remember that your brother has something against you*, but such people act as if it says, *If you . . . remember that you have something against your brother.* The passage means that it is so essential that brethren should dwell together in unity that even if at the place of worship you remember that you have given your brother some cause of offense, you are immediately to go and remove it by confession – and until this is done, God will not accept your worship.

In this case, it would be a brother having something against you, and not your having something against a brother, that would be a cause of staying away until reconciliation had taken place. When Christ spreads His table, it is your duty to be there no matter who is there. Of course, you are to use your influence for the purity of the church, and the Master has laid down the proper way in which this is to be done; but forsaking Communion is not that way.

> If a person has an important meeting at a bank, he will not neglect it because the weather is a little too cold or too hot, or because the clouds threaten rain.

## Meet on the Lord's Day

Now that you are a member of the body of Christ, let me earnestly exhort you to be punctual in attending the meetings. There are some who make excuses for any little thing for not meeting with other Christians on the Lord's Day. They will be about their business on Saturday and on Monday no matter what the weather is, but they will stay home on the Lord's Day, giving excuses that they would be ashamed to present to their fellow men, and that they will be ashamed to present to the great Judge.

If a person has an important meeting at a bank, he will not neglect it because the weather is a little too cold or too hot, or because the clouds threaten rain. No, he will go forth with energy and attend to his business; yet the same person will make these things an excuse for not going to the house of God and paying his vows to the Most High.

I knew a lady who would excuse herself from going out more than once on the Lord's Day, saying that she could not go out evenings, and yet she would go out to parties, concerts, or lectures two or three evenings a week. Do such people think that God is going to be mocked in this way? *Do not be deceived, God is not mocked* (Galatians 6:7).

Listen to the language of one who had erred in this way, but repented:

> A Sabbath at home, how unlike one spent in the courts of the Lord! I become restless – feel that something is wanting – my mind wanders – weariness pervades the body, and I am tempted to seek relief in sleep. I am unusually troubled with worldly thoughts and find a strong temptation to read something not appropriate to the day, to engage in worldly conversation, to work at my business, or to visit my neighbor. A Sabbath at home is to me a Sabbath lost. I tried it once and dread its influence, but I have learned something. Other men are like myself. Now I see why some of my fellow Christians have so little religious enjoyment, knowledge, and

influence. They are frequently absent from the house of God. Who can afford to lose a single Sabbath? Yet how many, many such precious days are lost, and worse than lost, in this land of Sabbaths!

Make a good beginning in this respect. Be punctual in meeting with other Christians to worship on the Lord's Day and to pray together during the week. Every pastor has members of his flock whom he can calculate with certainty upon seeing when they meet together to seek God. He can depend upon them. They make their plans by putting God first, arranging everything else around their spiritual duties. If visitors call on the evening of the prayer meeting, they will ask them to go with them or ask to be excused for an hour so that the precious opportunity may not be lost.

> Be punctual in meeting with other Christians to worship on the Lord's Day and to pray together during the week.

There are others whose attendance is sporadic and uncertain. They permit every little thing to act as a hindrance in their way. If some notable lecturer is to speak, some popular singer is to appear, or a political meeting is to be held, they are off in full pursuit of the amusement, while the prayer meeting is cast to the side as unimportant.

If the pastor acted in this way, they would be the first to complain, but is there one Bible for the pastor and another for the members? If it is the pastor's duty to preach, it is the duty of the members to be there to hear him. If the pastor is to lead the prayer meeting, it is the duty of every member to be there to sustain it. The same precious blood was shed for both, and they are both laid under the same law of love. *Let us consider how to stimulate one another to love and good deeds, not forsaking our own assembling together, as is the habit of some, but encouraging one another; and all the more as you see the day drawing near* (Hebrews 10:24-25).

Such people little know how much they lose by their neglect of the means of grace. An old Christian lady was very regular in her attendance at church, and when asked why she was always there before the service began, she said that the Lord had promised to be there and meet with her, but that He had not said in what part of the service He would come – in the first hymn or in the first prayer, in the reading of the Scriptures or in the sermon – and therefore she resolved to be present the whole time so that she might not lose the blessing. She also remarked that she did not like to come late to the house of God, for she did not want to disturb the worship of other people.

What a blessing Thomas lost by not being present with the other disciples in the upper room when our Lord appeared to them after His resurrection and said, *Peace be with you* (John 20:19). Of course, we do not know the reason why Thomas was not there, but as he was evidently in a dark, unbelieving state of mind, it is likely that he could have been there if he had wanted to be. He lost a most precious blessing to his soul by his neglect, and when the brethren next met him and began to tell him in glowing terms what a good meeting they had and how the Lord had appeared to them, he didn't believe what they said, but responded, *Unless I see in His hands the imprint of the nails, and put my finger into the place of the nails, and put my hand into His side, I will not believe* (John 20:25).

## Christian brotherly love

Another thing that I would urge upon the young convert is to cultivate a spirit of love toward every member of the body of Christ. This is a mark of true discipleship. *We know that we have passed out of death into life, because we love the brethren* (1 John 3:14). *By this all men will know that you are My disciples, if you have love for one another* (John 13:35). You ought to promote the spirit of love by the display of a loving and affectionate disposition. I would not want to disturb the harmony of the church of Christ for the whole world. Woe to the person by whom such offenses come! There are people who are very sensitive and suspicious and are constantly taking offense at their brethren where no offense was intended. They will say harsh and bitter things, but do not imitate them or contend with them. It takes two to make a quarrel, and by showing them a more excellent way, you may win them to a more lovely spirit. *You who are spiritual, restore such a one in a spirit of gentleness* (Galatians 6:1).

I was much impressed with a remark made by the Duke of Wellington in one of his letters: "I am not in the habit of deciding upon matters hastily or in anger; and the proof of this is that I never had a quarrel with any man in my life." This is a remarkable statement coming from one who had passed through such a long and public career and who had been brought in contact with all kinds of men.

If Christian faithfulness requires you to notice offenses committed against the laws of Christ by a member of the church, be sure that you go to work according to the rules laid down by the Lord in the eighteenth chapter of Matthew:

> *If your brother sins, go and show him his fault in private; if he listens to you, you have won your brother. But if he does not listen to you, take one or two more with you, so that by the mouth of two or three witnesses every fact may be confirmed. If he refuses to listen to them, tell it to the church; and if he refuses to listen even to the church, let him be to you as a Gentile and a tax collector.* (Matthew 18:15-17)

Do not whisper the offense to someone as a big secret, who, unable to keep the secret himself, will pass the secret on to others, and thus the matter will be talked about all over before you have an opportunity of seeing the offending brother himself. I have known a world of trouble brought upon churches by such blundering. Go to the offender at once, and let the matter be talked of between him and you alone. Do not go in a proud, domineering, superior spirit, or else you will be sure to fail in winning your brother. Like produces like, and a bitter, haughty spirit on your part will produce a bitter, haughty response on his part. Go in the spirit of love and of prayer, remembering that you are yourself imperfect and liable to fall.

If you do not succeed in winning your brother on your own, then you must take another brother with you. Try to get the most spiritual, loving, and prayerful brother you can find in the church. If you both fail in bringing the offender to repentance, then you must bring the matter before the entire church, but do not be ready to take offense. Do not make yourself out to be a kind of detective or spy in the church. Prevention is better than cure. Aim to keep up the spirit of vital Christianity so as to prevent backsliding in your own heart and in the hearts of others.

## Faithful stewards

Allow me to share with you another point before closing this chapter, and that is to make it a matter of conscience to bear your share of the financial burdens of the church, according as the Lord has prospered you. To build churches and to keep them in proper repair and order, to pay the pastor's salary punctually, and to carry on the benevolent enterprises of the church costs something, and every member is under obligation to bear his full proportion of that cost. To unite with any organization and enjoy the full advantages of it, and yet do nothing to help sustain it, would be regarded as supremely unfair, even by worldly men.

One man was told that a certain rich man had been converted. He asked, "Is his wallet converted?" The person who is really consecrated to Christ will be willing to make financial sacrifices to promote His cause.

Let what you do for the support of the cause of truth be done spontaneously and promptly. Do not require Christian leaders to ask and urge you again and again. Do not require them to waste their time in finding you. These brethren collect the funds for carrying on the affairs of the church voluntarily, and none but those who have tried it can tell what a laborious work it is. It is often made more difficult than it needs to be by the carelessness of some brethren. I have known a deacon to call at a brother's office four times to collect his promised support without finding him in, and yet that brother passed by the deacon's residence every day and could have saved all this trouble by giving what he had promised. When the collection is made for the missionary society and you happen to be absent that day, do not let the cause of missions suffer because you missed the collection, but give as soon as you can. Act from principle and give as in your Master's sight.

The following statement by a pastor illustrates this point:

> A short time ago, Pastor A. presented to my people the needs of one of our great benevolent societies, and on Monday I went with him to visit several members

of the congregation. Entering the office of a merchant, the following interview occurred:

Pastor A.: Good morning, Mr. B. Our openings for usefulness are multiplying, and we can most profitably use on the field of our labors all that is given to us.

Mr. B.: I am always glad to see you, Pastor A., and to do what I can for your noble society (handing him a liberal donation). We should all feel that we are only stewards of what God has given to us, and we should be diligent in doing good while we can.

Pastor A.: Thank you, Mr. B. We know you are a faithful friend, and so is your business partner, Mr. C. Is he in this morning?

Mr. B.: No, sir; he is in Europe. He was unexpectedly called to France on business, and sailed on a ship a few weeks ago. He plans to be gone about six months.

Pastor A.: Then I suppose we will not receive help from him this year.

Mr. B.: No, sir. But one of the last things he did before sailing was to ask me to attend to his charities with the same care as to his other business, and to give for him to the various objects of benevolence, as they are presented to our group of Christians, about the same amounts that he gave last year, or even to give more, as this year we have prospered. Do you remember how much he gave last year?

Pastor A.: One thousand dollars.

Mr. B.: Well, here is a check for fifteen hundred dollars, which I think is about what he would give if he were at home.

If all professing Christians were to act like that, under the eye of the Savior, remembering that they are but stewards of His money, giving according to this system and principle, there would soon be no lack of funds to carry out the plans of the largest benevolence!

## Chapter 5

## Duties to the Pastor

The relation between a Christian pastor and his people is represented in the Scriptures as very solemn and tender. A pastor is God's messenger, to speak to his people the words of truth, to feed their souls with the bread of life, and to watch over their souls as one who is soon to give an account to Him who sent him. He is to speak to them the truth in love, and not allow sin to pass unrebuked, regarding neither the frowns nor the smiles, the cheering nor the derision of those around him. He is to seek, above all things, their edification and spiritual profit, to study to build them up in faith and knowledge, and to have no greater joy than to see his spiritual children walking in the truth. *I have no greater joy than this, to hear of my children walking in the truth* (3 John v. 4).

On the other hand, his people are to esteem him very highly in love for his work's sake. They are to give him a place in their hearts and in their prayers. They are to defend his reputation, to submit to his authority (as long as it is scriptural), to provide for his temporal wants as long as he gives himself wholly to the Lord's work, and to greatly honor the message that he brings them from God.

## Affection

The relation of the pastor and a flock is such that it should last for life, unless dissolved by some very distinct and plain providence, in which the will of the great Head of the church will be clearly seen. The modern idea of hiring a pastor for a year, just as a farmer hires a man for his harvest work, so much work for so much pay, and then dismissing him when a few light-minded people claim to be dissatisfied and want a change, is a complete mockery of the apostolic relation of pastor and people.

> Give your pastor your love and confidence.

Give your pastor your love and confidence. It is natural that you should be deeply attached to that minister under whose preaching you were brought to the knowledge of the truth as it is in Jesus. It is all very natural and proper that you should like his preaching best and that you should feel a warm glow of emotion at the very mention of his name after he has passed on to the next life. No minister of good sense will feel offended, but rather pleased, to hear Christians speak kindly of their former pastors. However, when converts set up a particular minister as an idol in their souls, when they speak as if they could not get any good instruction under any preaching but his, when no prayers can lead their devotions heavenward but his, and when they refuse to give their affection and confidence to any other servant of the Lord Jesus, they show that their religion is of a very superficial character, and they justify serious doubts that they are converts of man rather than converts of Christ.

## Appreciation

No matter what pastor God in His providence places you under, if he is a good man, give him your sincere confidence and cooperation. He may not be as talented and eloquent as some others, for God in His sovereign goodness has given a variety of gifts to His ministers, but he is God's messenger to you, and it is at the peril of your soul that you despise his message. By careful study of the Word of God, he has prepared his sermons with great mental toil and has poured his soul out in prayer over them, and there is good for your soul in them if you will only place your mind in a proper attitude. Yours should not be the spirit of continual criticism and faultfinding, but that of earnest thirsting after truth, saying, *Speak, LORD, for Your servant is listening* (1 Samuel 3:9).

Professing Christians will sometimes go home from the house of God, and in the presence of their children and of the unsaved will utter the most unmerciful criticisms upon their pastor and his public efforts, and then wonder that their children are not converted! In the great day of God, it may be found that they have been the murderers of their children's souls by filling their minds with prejudice against the truth and its messenger.

Go to the pastor in all your spiritual difficulties, and make him the confidant of your soul's experiences. A good and godly pastor will be able to cheer and encourage you, and will make the truth, in its beautiful adaptations, to bear upon your case. When you receive good under his ministry, do not be afraid to mention it to him. It will not make him proud, but will cheer and encourage him. When anyone seems convicted of sin under his preaching, bring the case to his attention so that it can be made a matter of special prayer and inquiry.

You will thus become a coworker with your pastor, and he needs such people to help him. There is no work on earth so solemn and responsible, and none that so completely strains a man's best powers. None but those who have been called to the work can tell the care and anxiety that fill the faithful pastor's heart, often chasing sleep from his pillow for whole nights. Resolve that if you cannot lighten these cares, at least you will not intentionally add to their number. God may bless you for His servant's sake.

## Prayer

Let me urge you once again to pray for your pastor. I am aware that this may seem to be a very common remark, but prayer is no common thing. More depends upon this than we have even imagination to conceive of. See with what earnestness the apostles urged the churches to pray for them, showing what an important matter they regarded it!

A minister is set up in a prominent position. His every action and movement are watched and talked about. He is a target set up for every gossiping and malignant tongue to shoot at. He is a man with similar passions as others, exposed to distinct temptations, and Satan knows that if he can cause him to fall, the injury done to the cause of truth will be very great. We may be sure, therefore, that the Enemy will try every hellish dart to bring him down. He needs the prayers of God's people as a man, that more than common supplies of grace may be given to him, that he may be an example to the flock and will be of good report to all.

He also needs the prayers of the faithful as a minister, that the Holy Spirit may be with him in his studies and in his public duties. If the Holy Spirit is not with him, his best efforts will utterly fail. The attention of sinners will not be captured, and their minds will grow darker and their hearts harder under the preaching of the Word. The church will not be interested in the ways and the work of God as they ought, and the sad spectacle of a lukewarm congregation will be exhibited in the sight of God, angels, and men. Can there be any sight more heartrending to a truly godly minister while preaching those great truths that thrill all heaven with delight, than to see some people sleeping, some yawning, some gazing thoughtlessly around, and some frequently consulting their watches, as if thinking more of their dinners than the great business of the sanctuary? All this is often seen, though, even when the sermon is able and eloquent and when the best part of the week has been given to its preparation.

If the Spirit of God is poured out, though, under the same sermon, what a different state of things! A deep solemnity pervades the house, every eye is fixed upon the preacher, tears stream down many faces, that old hardened sinner trembles so that he can scarcely keep his seat, and that old saint seems ready to shout aloud, *This is the LORD'S doing; It is marvelous in our eyes* (Psalm 118:23)! One mighty wave of salvation rolls over the congregation, and preacher and people separate, feeling that it was good to be there. This is the state of things that God gives to a praying people – to a people who plead and wrestle before God in private for their minister.

On this subject, Charles G. Finney[8] says:

> I have seen Christians who would be in an agony when the minister was going into the pulpit, for fear his mind would be in a cloud, or his heart cold, or he would have no unction, and so a blessing should not come. I have labored with a man of this sort. He would pray until he got assurance in his mind that God would be with me in preaching, and sometimes he would pray

---

[8] Charles Finney (1792-1875) was an American preacher and evangelist and was one of the leaders of the Second Great Awakening.

himself sick. I have known the time when he has been in darkness for a season, while the people were gathering, and his mind was full of anxiety, and he would go again and again to pray, till finally he would come into the room in a more-peaceful state, and say, "The Lord has come, and He will be with us." And I do not know that I ever found him mistaken.

Finney also says:

I have known a church bear their minister on their arms in prayer from day to day, and watch with anxiety unutterable to see that he has the Holy Ghost with him in his labors! When they feel and pray thus, oh, what feelings and what looks are manifest in the congregation! They have felt anxiety unutterable to have the Word come with power and take effect, and when they see their prayer answered, and they hear a word or a sentence come warm from the heart and taking effect among the people, you can see their whole souls look out of their eyes. How different is the case where the church feels that the minister is praying, and so there is no need of their praying! They are mistaken. The church must desire and pray for the blessing. God says He will be inquired of *by the house of*

*Israel.* I wish you to feel that there can be no substitute for this.

*Thus says the Lord GOD, This also I will let the house of Israel ask Me to do for them: I will increase their men like a flock. Like the flock for sacrifices, like the flock at Jerusalem during her appointed feasts, so will the waste cities be filled with flocks of men. Then they will know that I am the LORD* (Ezekiel 36:37-38).

## Loyal to God's servant

Do not allow yourself to be made a part of any scheme against the pastor. If for any reason a minister's usefulness in a place has come to an end and it is thought that he ought to leave and that the good of the church requires it, then let the leading men of the church, whom he knows have been his true friends, go to him in a straightforward Christian spirit and tell him so. In nearly every instance, the separation will be carried out without difficulty.

Unfortunately, in some churches there are men who will not pursue a straightforward way if they can find a crooked one. They will pull strings, plot, form parties, and seek the removal of a minister when the highest interests of the church require that he should remain. Some do it from the mere love of change, others because they have a friend whom they want to get into the pastoral office, some because some outsider has become offended with the minister, and still others because the truth spoken has pinched their consciences.

My dear reader, have nothing to do with these plotters. The whole thing is wicked in its inception and execution. God must frown upon it, and He will visit with a fearful "Woe" those by whom such offenses come. Let the following statement by one who has had experience in this matter teach its own lesson. He says:

> Many years ago, I was drawn into a scheme to uproot one of God's servants from the field in which God had planted him. I and the men who led me – for I admit that I was foolish and was used by them – flattered ourselves that we were conscientious. We thought that we were doing God service when we drove that holy man from his pulpit and his work, and we said that we considered his labors ended in our town where I then lived.
>
> We complained because there was no revival, while we were gossiping, criticizing, and crushing instead of upholding by our efforts and our prayers the instrument at whose hand we harshly demanded the blessing. Well, he could not drag on the chariot of salvation with half a dozen of us taunting him with his weakness while we hung on as a dead weight to the wheels. He

did not have the power of the Spirit and could not convert people, so we haunted him like a deer, until, torn and bleeding, he fled into a covert to die.

Scarcely had he gone, when God came among us by His Spirit to show that He had blessed the labors of His dear, rejected servant. Our own hearts were broken and our wayward children converted, and I resolved at a convenient season to visit my former pastor, confess my sin, and thank him for his faithfulness to my wayward sons, who, like long-buried seeds, had now sprung up. But God denied me that relief that He might teach me a lesson every child of His ought to learn – that he who touched one of His servants touched the apple of His eye.

I heard that my old pastor was ill, and taking my son with me, I set out on a twenty-five-mile ride to see him. It was evening when I arrived, and his wife, with a feeling that was natural and excusable toward one who had so wronged her husband, denied me admittance to his chamber. She said (and her words were as arrows to my soul), "He may be dying, and the sight of your face might add to his anguish!"

*Has it come to this*, I said to myself, *that the man whose labors had, through Christ, brought me into His fold, whose hands had buried me in baptism, who had consoled my spirit in a terrible bereavement, and who had, until plotting men had alienated us, been to me as a brother – that this man could not die in peace with my face before him? God pity me!* I cried, "What have I done?"

I confessed my sin to that meek woman and implored her, for Christ's sake, to let me kneel before His dying servant and receive his forgiveness. I would gladly have taken his whole family to my home forever, as my own flesh and blood, but no such happiness was before me.

As I entered the room of the blessed warrior, whose armor was just falling from his limbs, he opened his languid eyes and said, "Brother Lee! Brother Lee!"

I bent over him and sobbed out, "My pastor!"

Then raising his white hand, he quoted Psalm 105:15 in a deep, impressive voice: *Do not touch My anointed ones, and do My prophets no harm.*

I spoke tenderly to him, telling him I had come to confess my sin and to bring some of his fruit to him, calling my son to tell him how he had found Christ. But he was unconscious of everything around him. The sight of my face had brought the last pang of earth to his spirit.

I kissed his brow and told him how dear he had been to me. I craved his pardon for my unfaithfulness and promised to care for his widow and fatherless little ones; but his only reply, murmured as if in a troubled dream, was, *Do not touch My anointed ones, and do My prophets no harm.*

I stayed by him all night, and at daybreak I closed his eyes. I offered his widow a house to live in the remainder of her days, but she said, "I freely forgive you, but my children, who entered deeply into their father's anguish, will never see me so regardless of his memory as to take anything from those who caused it. He has left us all with his covenant God, and He will care for us."

Those dying words sounded in my ears from that coffin and that grave. When I slept, Christ stood before me in my dreams, saying, *Do not touch My anointed ones, and do My prophets no harm.* These words followed me until I realized fully the esteem in which Christ holds those men who have given up all for His sake, and I vowed to love them evermore for His sake, even if they were not perfect. Since that day, I have talked less than before and have supported my pastor, even if he is not a very extraordinary man. My tongue shall cleave to the roof of my mouth, and my right hand forget its cunning (Psalm 137:5-6), before I dare to put asunder what God has joined together (Mark 10:9).

The above narrative was spoken to one who had approached him to help in trying to convince a pastor to resign. He told the story and then added, "I will not join you in the scheme that brought you here, and moreover, if I hear another word of this from your lips, I will ask my brethren to deal with you as with those who cause divisions. I would give all I own to recall what I did thirty years ago. Stop where you are, and pray to God, if perhaps the thought of your heart may be forgiven you."

## Be helpful to God's servant

There are many ways in which you can help your pastor in his solemn and responsible work. A very distinguished and successful minister said that a poor old lady in his church helped him to preach more than all the books in his library. She was always in her place in the house of God and was so deeply attentive that she scarcely lifted her eyes from his face from the beginning to the close of his sermon. When he would bring out some sweet promise or a rich expression of gospel truth, her countenance would light up with joy and her whole manner would show that she was enjoying a feast at the banqueting table of God. When the weather was depressing, the congregation small, or bodily weakness made him feel as if he could scarcely preach at all, the sight of that one hearer's eager and expectant face would rouse up his whole soul. Sometimes in his study, when he was tempted to take, for the next Sunday morning, some speculative theme in which he might display his learning, the thought of that old lady would call him back to the rich pastures of the gospel, for he felt that she would be disappointed with her Lord's Day feast.

By a punctual attendance upon the prayer meetings of the church, and promptly taking part in the services, you can greatly aid your pastor. Many stay away from these meetings altogether, and many who attend embarrass the pastor very much by their way of conducting themselves. They will come late, slide away into some corner as much out of sight as possible, see the meeting dragging along for lack of someone to take part, and yet they keep their seats and do nothing to promote the interest of the meeting. Yet such people will be the first to complain of the meetings being dull.

Anything worth doing at all is worth doing well. Go to the meeting early. Go forward near where the

> Anything worth doing at all is worth doing well.

pastor is, as if you felt identified with the people of God and with the welfare of Zion. Do not allow long pauses to throw a damper upon the meeting, but be always ready to speak and pray – and encourage others to do the same – so that the whole time of the meeting may be taken up. All this will cheer and comfort the pastor, and what is far more important, it will secure the approval of the gracious Savior, who, from His lofty seat in the heavens, is looking down to see how you seek to do His will.

When your pastor feels it his duty faithfully to expose the sins of professing Christians and to pointedly speak to sinners, sustain him in it, even when the Word condemns you. He is God's servant, and at the peril of his soul he must preach what his Master directs him to preach.

A minister was once asked not to preach so hard, for he was told that if he did, certain people would leave the church.

"Is not the preaching true?" he asked.

"Yes."

"Does not God bless it?"

"Yes."

"Did you ever see God work in this place like this before?

"No, I never did."

"Well," said the minister, "the devil has sent you to me, to get me to let down the tone of my preaching so as to ease the minds of the ungodly."

The man accepted the rebuke, and never afterward complained of plain preaching.

# Chapter 6

# Duties in Sunday School

It is the invariable desire of all true converts to do something to glorify Christ. They desire to see others enjoy the joy and peace that they have themselves experienced, and having been led to feel the value of their own souls, they intensely desire the salvation of the souls of others. Every soul that knows Jesus will desire to work for Jesus, and the honest, spontaneous cry of the renewed heart is, *Lord, what wilt thou have me to do?* (Acts 9:6 KJV).

## Teach

In looking for a field in which to labor for Christ, you will find a most useful and suitable one in the Sunday school. God alone can tell and eternity alone can unfold the good that has been done by this institution. It was a happy day for the church and a happy day for the world when Robert Raikes conceived the idea of gathering the children together on the Lord's Day "to hear of heaven, and learn the way." He had little idea of the great things that would grow out of such a small beginning, but those who are faithful in a few things, God will make rulers over many things (Matthew 25:23).

In giving an account of his first efforts, Robert Raikes says:

> The beginning of this scheme was entirely owing to accident. Some business leading me one morning into the suburbs of the city, where the lowest of the people, who are principally employed in the pin manufactory, chiefly reside, I was struck with concern at seeing a group of children, wretchedly ragged, playing in the street. I asked an inhabitant whether those children belonged to that part of the town, and I lamented their misery and idleness.
>
> "Ah, sir," said the woman to whom I was speaking, "if you would see this part of the town on Sunday, you would be shocked indeed, for then the street is filled with multitudes of these poor children who, released on that day from employment, spend their time in noise and riot, cursing and swearing, in a manner so shocking as to convey to any serious mind an idea of hell rather than of any other place. Upon the Lord's Day they are all given up to

> follow their inclinations without restraint, as their parents, totally abandoned themselves, have no idea of instilling into the minds of their children principles to which they themselves are entire strangers."

He then formed the first Sunday school in the world, and, after a three-year trial, he wrote to a friend, "I wish you were here to make inquiry into the effort. A woman who lives in a lane where I began a school told me some time ago that the place was quite a heaven on Sundays, compared to what it used to be. The number who have learned to read and say their catechism is so great that I am astonished at it."

From this small beginning the work spread, until in Great Britain there were about one million children in Sunday schools in the course of a few years. And now, in the United States and all over the world, millions of voices unite in singing, "I'm glad I'm in this army."

Though no one denies the good that these schools are doing, it is a sad fact that Sunday school superintendents often find it difficult to get enough teachers from the church to sustain them. You will sometimes find a church numbering three or four hundred members, yet their Sunday school really suffers for lack of teachers. This is a shame and a disgrace in the sight of the world, and must be highly displeasing to that blessed Savior who said, *Permit the children to come to Me, and do not hinder them, for the kingdom of God belongs to such as these* (Luke 18:16).

I hope that you will require no urging to engage

in this work, but that under a deep sense of duty and personal obligation to Him who bought you with His own blood, you will enter upon it with all your heart.

## Be tender and loving

In order that your mind may be suitably impressed with the importance of the work, think of the infinite value of the souls you are going to instruct. They are to live forever, and your words may make impressions that will last through eternal ages.

"Don't write there," someone said to a boy who was writing with a pin on a pane of glass in the window of a hotel.

"Why?" he asked.

"Because you can't rub it out," was the reply.

Remember that it is upon deathless spirits that you are writing and making impressions, and these impressions are to remain forever; they can never be rubbed out. Let this make you solemnly careful what thoughts you present to the minds of your young students. You are to meet them again at the judgment seat of God, and you must give a strict account of what you have spoken.

Seek to meet your class, therefore, with a tender, loving spirit – that spirit that brought Jesus from His throne in glory to suffer the agonies of the cross. There is a transforming, melting power in love that will be felt by the most careless and hardened people. A teacher who has prayed for his class and then comes to them with his heart full of love for their souls will have better order, better attention, and will do a thousand times

## DUTIES IN SUNDAY SCHOOL

more good than he who loses his temper and allows himself to indulge an angry spirit.

Let the following case illustrate this: Not long ago a gentleman visited a Sunday school, and being a little early, he looked around him. One class that he noticed had four boys in it. Soon their teacher, a tall, fine-looking young man came in, but with a downcast countenance. He took his seat with a cold, dismal, almost angry look. He seemingly paid no attention to the boys. A cap was knocked off the seat. That made some of the boys laugh. The teacher turned around, and said sharply, "Boys, be still!"

> Be kind and affectionate to your little students.

Soon something else caused the boys to laugh again. Moving quickly around the class, the teacher said, "Boys, I told you to be still!" His face again assumed its cold expression, now slightly tinged with irritation.

A third slight disturbance occurred, and with a look, voice, and manner decidedly angry, he said, "Boys, I tell you again to stop! I won't have this!"

It would be impossible for that teacher to do his class any good. It has been truly said that to make a child angry during his lesson, give him his food scalding hot. We must not forget that we were once children ourselves, and we had childish faults. We must remember that it can be difficult for the young to fix their minds for any great length of time upon serious things.

Make your instructions attractive by preparing yourself with illustrations suitable to the young mind. Study the lesson carefully and with all the aids you can find. Be kind and affectionate to your little students, and you will soon gain an influence over them that will be seen in its blessed results forever. If they are sick or in trouble, visit them at their homes. Show them that you are their best friend, and you will bind them to you for life. When I think of my Sunday school teacher, my heart leaps with gratitude, and there is no man in the world I would be more glad to see.

## Teach simple truths

Let your instructions be spiritual and practical, and such as will tend directly to the conversion of their souls. Dr. Payson[9] says:

"If God should place in your hand a diamond and tell you to inscribe on it a sentence that would be read at the last day, and shown there as an idea of your thoughts and feelings, what caution would you exercise in the selection! This is what God has done! He has placed before you immortal minds, more imperishable than the diamond, on which you are continually inscribing, by your spirit or example, something that will remain and will be exhibited for or against you at the judgment day."

There are some teachers whose instructions are almost entirely speculative – the wanderings of the children of Israel before reaching the promised land,

---

9   Edward Payson (1783-1827) was an American Congregationalist pastor. He was drawn to Jesus by reading *The Life and Diary of David Brainerd*. Payson was known for his intimacy with God and was known as "Praying Payson." His memoir, writings, and many of his sermons are still available today.

the description of the temple of Solomon, the journeys of the apostle Paul with a geographical account of the countries which he passed through and the cities he visited, together with curious questions to be solved from the Bible. Now I do not say that the knowledge of such things is not useful, but it does not tend to promote the highest object of Sunday school instruction – the conversion of the souls of the young. The illumination of the intellect is good in its place, but the heart must not be forgotten.

Remember that children are capable of conversion at a very early age. Timothy knew the Holy Scriptures from an early age: *From childhood you have known the sacred writings which are able to give you the wisdom that leads to salvation through faith which is in Christ Jesus* (2 Timothy 3:15).

I once knew a lady who, in her instructions, constantly aimed at the conversion of her class. It was her habit to pray for each one specifically, to visit them at their homes for Christian conversation, and to watch anxiously for any sign of the truth beginning to take effect. The result was that conversions were frequent among them. Teach your class how they can be saved from their lost and perishing condition. Hold up Christ before their young eyes in His saving power. The gospel, in its beautiful simplicity, is admirably adapted to the mind of the child as well as the philosopher. No matter what else you teach them, if you neglect this, you leave them destitute of eternal life.

A man who had recently been converted said to his minister, "Oh sir, give your congregation something to do that will make their peace with God, and you will please them mightily. It is just what people like. The biggest miser in the parish would pull out his wallet and give something to help build a church, and they would put a steeple on it that would reach up near the clouds, and even put a weathervane on top of it, if you would just tell them that it would help to save them. But people don't like to think that they can do nothing; and when they hear ministers preaching, *Believe in the Lord Jesus, and you will be saved* (Acts 16:31), they step over it, and over it, and miss it, perhaps, like me, for twenty-seven years; and some, I am afraid, even until they die."

## Punctuality

Another matter I would urge upon you is to be punctual and persevering in your attendance at Sunday school. One of the greatest difficulties that Sunday school superintendents have to contend with is the irregularity of teachers in their attendance. They will take a class and begin with great seeming earnestness, but in a few months their zeal begins to wane and they will be frequently absent, and might soon quit teaching the class altogether. I have seen a class of thoughtless boys far more punctual in their attendance than their teacher, and he was a professing Christian. This is a sad sight, and will do much harm to the cause of truth. My reader, I hope better things of you. Be in your place, at your post of duty, regularly, as the holy day of God dawns upon you. If you must be absent, state the reason

## DUTIES IN SUNDAY SCHOOL

to your class and introduce a friend to take your place until you return.

Do not give way to discouragement if you are not as successful as you had hoped. It is particularly a work of faith. You might be doing a great deal more good than you can see, and at any rate, it is your obligation to go on in the path of duty, sowing the seed and leaving the result with God.

"It is no use to try," said a young man. "They are so careless and unconcerned that I am quite sure that no good can be done."

An aged gentleman to whom the remark was made replied, "Such an argument would at one time have satisfied me; now, however, I can see its fallacy. It is forty years since I was first a Sunday school teacher, and the boys whom I taught seemed so perversely deaf to all my words that at length I considered myself justified in giving it up as a hopeless task. During the ensuing thirty years of my life, I continued uninterested in the cause of Sunday schools, until a circumstance occurred that led me to see my error and to return to my duty.

"One evening as I was returning from church, I was approached by a man who smiled in my face, and holding out his hand to me, inquired whether my name was Mr. P—. I answered that it was.

"'Do you remember,' he asked, 'a boy named Dempster who attended your Sunday school about thirty years ago?'

"'Dempster!' I said. 'I remember Tom Dempster very well. He was a very wild and wicked boy!'

"'I was that wild and wicked boy,' said the man, 'though now, thanks be to God, I am a very different person from what I was then. It was your instructions, blessed by God's Spirit, that brought conviction of the truth home to my mind, long after I had left your school.'"

The old gentleman said, as he concluded his statement, "My object since then has been to do my work and pray for the Spirit to do His."

> Ye who on each returning sacred day,
> > Circled by listening youthful groups are seen,
> Who pour instruction on the tender mind,
> > From the pure well-spring of eternal truth,
> In joyful hope pursue your work of love.
> > The Shepherd's eye, which watches all the lambs,
> Upon you smiles, His kind approval cheers.
> > Hands, which the temple of our God shall rear,
> 'Tis yours to guide and train to heavenly skill.
> > They whom benighted heathen tribes shall hail,
> > "How beauteous are their feet who publish peace,"
> > Learn from your lips salvation's joyful sound.[10]

---

10 From "The Sabbath School Teacher's Work" by A. B. H., published in *The Congregational Visiter*, Vol. 2, No. 4, April 1845.

## Chapter 7

## Duties in the World

When God converts someone, that person is no doubt that moment prepared for heaven. He is washed in the blood that cleanses from all sin, and by the righteousness of Jesus is fitted for the society of the sinless congregation above.

Why, then, is he not taken there at once? Because he has a work to do for others. He has a testimony to bear for the Lord Jesus and an example of holy consistency of life to show that may lead people to glorify his Father in heaven. He is to live for a purpose, to live in a way worthy of an immortal being – a probationer for eternity. He is to seek to be useful, and every day he lives he is to try and make the world better and happier for his having lived in it.

It is through God's people that He carries on the mighty purposes of His love on earth. When Christ fed the people in a miraculous manner with a few loaves, it is said that He gave the bread to the disciples, and they gave it to the multitude. It is still this way today. The body of Christ is the appointed instrument by which the Bread of Life is to be distributed to the nations of the earth.

## Be useful

We sometimes hear it said of a professing Christian, "He is a good man, but he is not a useful man." The wonder in such a case is how he can be said to be good at all! The great difficulty is that, in the opinion of many, showing a little kindness and having a few good feelings and benevolent emotions is called goodness. The truth is that if these are confined to the individual and do not bring forth fruits to bless the world, they become only a refined form of selfishness.

The great reason why God converts a soul is not merely to secure the salvation of an individual, but also to start him on a career of usefulness that may bring forth blessed results, lasting for all eternity. This is why Christians in their new life are said to be *created in Christ Jesus for good works* (Ephesians 2:10). They are as much made to be useful as the sun is made to shine or as the air is made to be breathed. It is not enough that we *cease to do evil*, but we must also *learn to do good* (Isaiah 1:16-17).

> If a professing Christian is not a useful person, it becomes a very serious question whether he is a Christian at all.

If a professing Christian is not a useful person, it becomes a very serious question whether he is a Christian at all. The great Master, whose name he bears, went about constantly doing good. To do good to others was the delight of His soul. It was His meat and His drink. By day and by night, in season and out of season, He was at this work of love. His followers walked in His footsteps. They did not merely leave us a record of their feelings, emotions, or opinions, but of the "Acts of the Apostles." A Christian in a truly healthy state of mind who took some time to rest at the end of a day in which he had done nothing for Jesus, would be unable to find true rest. Instead, he would be disturbed by the groans and cries of those who are ready to perish, and he would get up from his unrefreshing pillow, resolved to work while it is called today.

## Do something

Suppose that you are sitting in your own comfortable home after the work and the cares of the day are over. The shadows of evening are gathering around you. All nature is calm and serene. As the setting sun lights up the clouds into ever-varying and fantastic forms, gilding every object around you with its departing glory, you feel your mind drawn into a solemn, meditative mood, and you are lifted "from nature up to nature's God."[11]

Then you look up and see a stranger approaching your dwelling. His first appearance awes and impresses you. His look is grave and serious. His countenance displays tenderness and benevolence. His apparel is

---

11   This quote likely came from *Luther: Or, The Spirit of the Reformation*, a book-length poem by English poet and pastor Robert Montgomery (1807-1855).

plain and travel-worn, but there is a holy dignity about Him that makes you feel as you never did in any mortal presence before. A tear trembles in His eye and rolls down His expressive face, while His bosom heaves under emotions too big for utterance. He speaks – and His words are words of fire that burn into your soul! His thoughts thrill your heart and exert an unearthly influence upon you. The things of eternity, in their incredible grandeur, are brought near to you as living realities, and the world and its happiest scenes appear to be very empty things.

You are wondering who this Stranger is, when all at once your eyes are opened and you see that you are in the presence of the Man of Sorrows – your own Savior! As He did with Thomas, He shows you His hands and His side, and urges you to see there the evidences of His love. He fixes upon you that look that melted Peter's heart, and those eyes that swam in tears of anguish for you, and He asks if you love Him. You fall at His feet, exclaiming, "Blessed Savior, I do love You! O help me to love You more!"

Suppose, then, that He asks, as an evidence of your love to Him, that you go to those who are lacking the means of grace and tell them the story of His love, urging them in His stead to be reconciled to God. Like Moses, you plead your lack of eloquence and your inability to go under the circumstances in which you are placed. He then asks, if you are not able to go yourself, that you will contribute of your worldly means to send others who are able and willing to go. Now could you, in the presence of Him who agonized upon the cross for you and who is to put the crown of glory upon your head, refuse this most reasonable request?

Although Jesus is not in this way personally visiting us at our homes and appealing to our hearts, He is really doing so through the various organizations that He has instituted for proclaiming His truth abroad. From His throne in heaven He says, "Support them, and I will consider it as done to Myself." Standing upon the Mount of Olives, in view of the scenes of His rest and devotion and tragic sufferings, His farewell command was, *Go into all the world and preach the gospel to all creation* (Mark 16:15). This is binding upon every Christian.

> We must either go or send.

We must either go or send. We live in an age of special promise to the human family. In our own country, new and vast fields of exertion invite the energies of the people of God. Forms of error, with a zeal that rebukes us, are entering these fields. Infidelity in some of its most loathsome and dangerous forms is uttering its blasphemies against the Holy One, while the religion of mere form and ceremony plants itself everywhere to block up the pathway of true, vital godliness. Between these enemies of God, coming from opposite directions and with opposing watchwords, we are called to take our stand and present Christ's blessed gospel. It is ours to unfurl the banner that has been dipped in the blood shed for the ransom of a world, and to go forth to the holy conflict with an unwavering faith! It is amazing the amount of good that can be done by personal effort, if only the heart is truly alive to the work.

Two pious young men had a considerable distance to walk in order to reach their place of worship. They accordingly agreed to invite people, as they went along, to go to the house of God with them. They continued doing this, and eventually they counted no less than twenty people who had accepted their invitation, ten of whom were converted and became members of the church.

Another young man, by his own efforts, gathered together a class of twelve boys whom he instructed in the truths of the Bible on the Lord's Day. He went on in spite of all discouragements, making each member of his class a subject of prayer until every one of them was brought to Christ. Two of them are now ministers of the gospel, and several of them are teachers of the young.

The main thing is to be always active in the Master's service, watching for opportunities of doing good. Some people are ready to avail themselves of what promises to be some great occasion of usefulness, but they allow the little occasions that are occurring every hour of the day to pass by unnoticed. If we are working away for Jesus from the motive of love, no matter how small our sphere, we will be approved as much as the missionary who influences the destiny of a nation, or the martyr who honors the truth at the stake. It has been said that it is a great deal easier to die *once* for Christ than to live *always* for Him. It is easier to do some great act that will attract the attention of the world than to go on patiently plodding through the daily duties that fall in our way every hour.

Many souls whom the public preaching of the

Word fails to move can be reached by personal conversation. A gentleman went into a store one day to do some business, and he found the clerk alone. The clerk was a moral man and a regular church attender. The gentleman asked if he felt any anxiety about the salvation of his soul.

"I cannot say that I do," was the reply.

"You believe that, as a sinner, you cannot be saved in any way but through faith in Christ?"

"Yes, I believe it, but I do not feel it."

"Then you acknowledge that you are at risk to die and be lost at any moment?"

"Yes, I know that is so."

"Now then," said the gentleman, "you know your duty – to repent of sin and believe in Christ; will you begin this moment to do your duty as far as you know how?"

"I will," he replied.

In a few days that young man was a happy Christian. Many professing Christians would have let that opportunity of doing good pass by, and through such neglect, that soul might have been lost.

## Tactfulness

I want to deeply impress upon the mind of the young convert the importance of cultivating great skill and wisdom in speaking to sinners about their souls. Great harm may be done by a reckless and unwise mode of approach. There is such a thing as being wise to win souls. There is a certain skill and tact that some possess that we should seek to imitate. Let the following fact help to illustrate this.

A very wicked, quick-tempered man became a neighbor to a devoted minister of the gospel. He began a career of sin, and he declared his intent to insult the minister if he would attempt to speak to him. After a little while, the hardened man was taken down by a severe sickness, and the minister resolved to go and see him.

"If you do, he will insult you," said the friend who had informed him of the man's sickness.

"I will see him, nevertheless, and look to God for guidance and blessing," replied the minister.

Accordingly, he called and inquired of the sick man about his health. He received very abrupt and almost uncivil replies. However, without saying one word on Christianity, he opened his Bible and said, "If you do not object, I will read to you." He read the fifteenth chapter of Luke, offered a short prayer, and left.

The next day he again visited, read the fifty-third chapter of Isaiah, prayed, and left as before, without saying a word of his own. He continued doing this for some time, until one day the hardened sinner broke completely down, grasped the minister's hand, wept, confessed himself a sinner, and said he was a wonder to himself.

"It is God," replied the minister. "I have not spoken a word. God has spoken. He has done this."

"Yes," said the man. "I see it now. If you had spoken a single word of your own to me when you first came, or for some time after, I would not have tolerated it.

As weak as I was, I would have tried to turn you out of my house. I was astonished at your daring to come to me. You took me by surprise. I could not be angry when you asked in such a kind way about my health. You read me those beautiful words. I knew they were not your words, but God's own words, and I was silent. You shut the Book, and I thought you would begin to reproach me and tell me what a sinful wretch I was, and that would be my time to speak; but I looked up and saw you on your knees and heard you praying for me, and then, without one word, you were gone."

We have here a proof of great tact and good judgment – a union of zeal and knowledge that is beautiful to look upon and worthy of imitation. When a sinner is angry or excited by intoxicating liquor, or when he is in the presence of his wicked companions, it will often do more harm than good to speak to him about Christianity or rebuke him for his sins. To then enter into discussion with him on some matter of controversy is improper. By getting the sinner alone, speaking to him in love, pressing the truth solemnly upon his conscience, and speaking briefly, you can expect the Holy Spirit to bless your efforts. Oh, what a matter of eternal joy it is to win one soul to Jesus!

> Oh, what a matter of eternal joy it is to win one soul to Jesus!

## Wisdom

In conversing with people who are inquiring about their souls, much prudence is required. Great care should be taken that the mind is not diverted from the necessity of an immediate trust in Christ. When the mind is in a spiritually awakened state, it is ready to seek comfort anywhere but in the right place – in anything or anyone but Jesus.

I read somewhere of a young lady who believed that she was a lost sinner. She was in agony of mind and could find no relief. She had a pious brother who was away from home at the time, and she began to entertain the feeling that she should wait until he came home, and then he would help her to come to Jesus.

When the brother came home, he was informed of the state of things, and he made up his mind to go to his own room without seeing her; but as he passed the door of her room, she ran out and grabbed hold of him, crying out, "Oh, brother, save me! Save me! If you don't, I will die!"

The brother reflected a moment, and then pushing her away almost roughly, yet with a voice trembling with affection, said, "So you will come to *me* rather than to Jesus! I can do nothing at all for you."

And so, left to herself, her false refuge having been torn away, she felt that all her trouble had been because she was unwilling to come to Christ, and in a short time she surrendered to Him and was at peace.

## Chapter 8

# Enemies of Grace

Everything good in this world of sin and depravity has foes to encounter that aim at its destruction. This is especially true of grace in the heart. It did not grow up there naturally of itself, but it had to be planted by the divine hand. The same power that put it there must keep it there; the same agency that gave spiritual life must sustain that life. Nevertheless, we must be coworkers with God in this work. We must watch as well as pray against the approach of every spiritual foe. We must not pray against temptation and then run into it. We must not ask for spiritual health and then swallow spiritual poison. Whatever we find to be an enemy to the work of God in our souls, we must be ready to sacrifice, even if it is as dear to us as a right hand or a right eye.

## Amusements

One thing that greatly tends to destroy the life of God in the souls of many young converts is the rage for amusement that abounds in the present day. Unconverted people are called *lovers of pleasure rather than lovers of God* (2 Timothy 3:4). This is the object for which they live. This is the meaningless, selfish purpose to which they give up their whole being. This is to be expected from them, and we are not surprised by it. However, when those who profess to be dead to the world with Christ and claim to have risen with Him into a new life join with the world in their amusements until both get blended together and the distinction between the world and the church is nearly lost, then there is reason, not merely for astonishment, but for the deepest alarm.

Allow me to say that I am no enemy to recreations and innocent amusements. The mind of man is not made to be always working hard. Some people should take time off more than they do, and enjoy the beauty of nature and the joys of family and friendships. There is a time to laugh as well as a time to weep (Ecclesiastes 3:4). It has been said that Jesus wept, but never laughed. This I do not believe. He was not only God, but was also man, and it is a part of man's nature to laugh as well as to weep. It is true that we have no account of Him laughing, and neither do we have accounts of many other things that doubtless He did, as man. To laugh is not sinful, unless we are laughing at sin. The religion of superstition is always gloomy, but the religion of Christ is cheerful and fills the soul with gladness. Still, all this is no plea for Christians indulging in worldly and sinful amusements. Our Christianity is to regulate our recreations as well as everything else.

## Religious entertainment and raffles

There are few things that tend to hurt the spirituality of Christians in the present day more than those religious festivals and bazaars organized for the purpose of supporting some religious and benevolent object. The object to be accomplished is so good and the motive of many of those who take part in them is so just, that people get blinded to the many great evils connected with them. These evils are allowed under a religious name and under a religious sanction so that conscience is confused and seduced and ceases to rightly perform its functions – and the young Christian is betrayed into calling evil good.

In former times, if Christians wanted to build a place of worship or pay off a debt upon one already built, they put their hands in their pockets and paid it. If voluntary aid could be obtained from God's people, good and well; but they never thought of getting up an entertainment that would please the ungodly and compromise the dignity of truth for the pitiful purpose of getting a little money from the hands of the wicked. No; they would have worshipped God in a barn or in a log schoolhouse all their days rather than have done so!

To see God's professed people – respectable married women, old men, church officers, and young Christians – participate in parades and theatrical performances and dress up in some absurd style for the purpose of amusing a staring crowd is most mortifying and distressing to sincere, thoughtful Christians. Then, I am told, sometimes the whole event ends with a raffle, which everybody knows is a type of gambling. Oh, it was a sad sight to see the wicked gambling for our Lord's garments at the foot of the cross, but it is still sadder to see professed Christians encouraging the same evil in the name of our holy religion! *Let my soul not enter into their council; Let not my glory be united with their assembly* (Genesis 49:6).

## Social extravagance and dance

The spirituality of individuals and churches is very much damaged in our cities and large towns by those fashionable parties that have come so much into style of late. These parties are often upon a scale of great extravagance and expense, quite inconsistent with the simplicity of Christ, and this evil increases as a rivalry gets up among the members of the church as to who will give the finest entertainment. The whole winter is taken up in a round of these assemblies, so that Christians will be called to attend two or three of them in a week. The entertainment continues to a very late hour, so that family worship is neglected in most of the homes of those who attend them, and it is to be feared that private worship is neglected too.

A winter spent in this kind of excess is sure to injure the devotional spirit and to break up those fixed habits of godliness that all those who profess

Christianity should form and preserve. Of course, I do not utter one word against social enjoyment with good Christians. We are made to be social beings, and many of the purest enjoyments of our lives spring from this source. Christianity, instead of repressing this part of our nature, directs, elevates, and refines it. But when our social feelings are indulged at the expense of the health of the soul, we may be sure that they have been carried too far.

One evil leads to another, and I have been told that these parties often end with dancing. Dancing in Christian homes and by Christian people! If you were suddenly struck with a fatal disease and eternal realities were to burst upon you as only a deathbed can reveal them, would you send for one of the worldly, dancing Christians to pray for you? Would someone spiritually awakened and seeking salvation go to one of these parties and ask, *What must I do to be saved?* (Acts 16:30). Dancing begun at these parties leads to more worldliness, worldly entertainment, desiring the pleasures of this world, and eventually, I'm afraid, to eternal damnation.

> One evil leads to another.

Take the following incident from the experience of a pastor: "A most interesting work of grace occurred in a Presbyterian church in this city. Many anxiously inquired what they should do to be saved. Among this number was a young lady who listened to the voice of truth and was troubled. Conscience spoke, and she felt the claims of God on her, but she could not now attend to the matters of her soul's salvation.

"One evening the meeting was more than usually interesting and solemn, but the next evening a party was to be held, and from this scene of solemnity she hurried away and joined in the frivolous dance. She tried to drown the admonitions of her conscience with the sound of the music, and for a little while she succeeded. Amid the display of fashion, the glare of lights, and the intoxication of the scene, her conscience slumbered and allowed the lighthearted transgressor to revel undisturbed in forbidden pleasure.

"But again, she felt herself as a sinner, and again she went to the meeting for conversation and prayer. Her heart was the seat of many painful emotions. The claims of truth and duty were urged. She *would* yield – she *would* follow the Savior – but the theater, the dancing, the music, her friends, how could she give these up?

"She was invited to attend another party, and she went. Satan, as an angel of light, shed a deceptive radiance over the scene. She tried to be happy. She tried to believe that her serious thoughts were melancholy and that she still had plenty of time to prepare for eternity. She returned to her home, but she returned to die – to die without hope. 'I did not think,' she said while dying, 'that I would have to die so soon.'

"One evening she was at the meeting concerned for her soul, and the next evening she was at the party with her friends, having a great time. A few nights more, and she was in her coffin! One week, with a heart light as air, she went to a store to buy new clothes to wear to the party. The next week her friends went to the same store to buy clothes to wear to her funeral."

I believe it was Richard Cecil[12] who, when traveling in a stagecoach, heard a young lady talking to her companion about an anticipated dance. "Oh!" she said, "I very much enjoy a dance. I enjoy the thought of its coming on, I enjoy the pleasure while it lasts, and I like to think of it after it is over!"

"I think, madam," said Mr. Cecil, "there is a fourth pleasure that you have forgotten to mention."

"Indeed, sir, I don't remember it. What do you refer to?"

"The pleasure it will afford you, madam, when you come to die."

The remark was an arrow sent by the Spirit of God, and it led to her conversion.

Just as Satan quoted Scripture even to our Lord, so do people quote the Bible to defend dancing. David dancing before the Lord as an expression of his joy when the ark of God was restored (2 Samuel 6:14) and Miriam dancing at the wonderful national deliverance at the Red Sea (Exodus 15:20) are often referred to. That was the mode in which the people of the East expressed their joy, just as rending their garments or throwing dust and ashes upon their heads was their mode of expressing sorrow. We have no instance of promiscuous dancing; whenever mentioned, the sexes are separate. This was the case with Miriam, and also in other places, when referred to. But to make these cases an excuse for the promiscuous intermingling of the sexes, the indecent dances of modern times, the

---

12  Richard Cecil (1748-1810) was an evangelical Anglican pastor in England.

shameless exposure of the body, the late hours, and the many other evils that attend the dance, is an insult to the sacred Scriptures and an outrage upon common sense. It is seeking to make the source of all truth and goodness responsible for error and wrong.

## Other worldly amusements

What can we say of professing Christians going to the theater, concerts, and other such places? The best that can be said of the theater is that it is a place of vain amusement. Recreations and amusements are sometimes necessary, and doubtless there are amusements in which good people can engage with the proper decency and morality and with benefit to themselves both physically and intellectually. But the theater is not one of them.

It has been well said, "Amusements must be blameless, as well as ingenious; safe, as well as rational; moral, as well as intellectual. Whatever pleasing idea, whatever fun sentiment, whatever cheery expression, should we not jealously watch against any unsoundness in the general principle, and mischief in the prevailing tendency?"

Tried by such a test, the theater is a place utterly unfit for good people to visit. It produces false principles of action and false views of life. It deadens all the finer feelings of our nature by making wounds, shrieks, groans, murders, and assassinations the subject of a pleasing excitement. In short, many of its most popular exhibitions are grossly immoral.

It is true that the theater has been called a school of morals, but it is easy to give the finest names to the vilest things. On this point, the Dr. Thompson of New York says:

> "If the theater is a place of wholesome moral influence – a school of virtue, as it is sometimes called – then it is proper for me as a Christian minister to frequent it and to urge my church to do so likewise. But this would be considered quite out of character by the majority of actors and actresses. Why? Not merely because of my profession, but because the theater is known to be an unfit place for any serious-minded person."

Some years ago, a clergyman residing in the vicinity of Boston visited a theater in that city in order to study the elocution of a distinguished actor. To avoid being recognized, lest his example should do harm, he took his seat in the pit with his hat drawn over his brow. But a jokester nearby soon discovered who he was, and when the curtain dropped, he peered under the embarrassed clergyman's hat, pronounced his name aloud with an oath and an exclamation of surprise, and then added, with mock gravity, "Let us pray!"

The effect was highly ridiculous. The audience was convulsed with laughter. But why so ridiculous? Is prayer a foolish thing? Is it absurd for a sinful, dependent creature to offer supplication to his Maker? No;

there is a great deal of solemn appealing to heaven even on the stage. Apart from the manner, it was the felt inappropriateness of the thing that provoked a laugh. The thought of prayer in such a place, the presence of a Christian minister, or of anyone making pretensions to piety amid such scenes, amused that pleasure-loving audience. That laugh disclosed the character of the place and the object of their assembling.

We can rest assured that where there is a desire for the excitement of worldly amusements, there is a very low state of Christianity in the soul, if there is any Christianity at all. The soul that lives near God has a fullness of joy and peace that is most satisfying. The soul that drinks of the river of life will not stoop to drink of the filthy puddles of sin. The heart in which Christ dwells has no room for His enemies.

> 'Tis not for man to trifle! Life is brief,
>     And sin is here.
> Our age is but the falling of a leaf,
>     A dropping tear.
> We have not time to sport away the hours,
> All must be earnest in a world like ours.[13]

---

[13] From "Our One Life" by Horatius Bonar (1808-1889).

## Chapter 9

# Helps and Hindrances in Daily Life

In your journey heavenward, your highest interest requires that you should avail yourself of all the helps you can, having your mind deeply impressed with your personal responsibility to God. A young Christian made this entry in his diary: "Resolved that I will, the Lord being my helper, think, speak, and act as an individual; for as such I must live, and as such I must die, stand before God, and be damned, or saved, forever and ever. I have been waiting for others; I must act as if I were the only one to act, and wait no longer."

## Personal devotion and dedication

This is just what is needed – not to be comparing ourselves with others, with the members and officeholders of the church, and setting them up as our standard, but each of us aiming at personal piety for ourselves. Each must work for God every day as if there were not another worker in the world.

One who knew Harlan Page well, said, "I have well considered the assertion when I say that during nine years in which we were associated in labors, I do not know that I ever talked with him long enough to have any interchange of thought and feeling in which I did not receive from him an impulse heavenward – an impulse onward in duty to God and the souls of men." He did not wait for the church to go to work before he would do anything, but he did his own work that lay around, as in God's sight.

It would be a great help to have special times set apart for the study of the Bible, accompanied with much earnest prayer for the sanctifying influences of the Holy Spirit.

We are not to look at the opinion of the world, the standard of piety in the church, or the attainments of deacons and ministers in personal religion, but we are to look at the rules that God lays down in the Scriptures. The Word of God demands a very high standard of spirituality, and God tells us that *the mind set on the Spirit is life and peace* (Romans 8:6). Nothing should be allowed to interfere with our hours of private devotion. It is the habit of some Christians to take, in the morning, a short portion of Scripture to meditate upon during the day, and amid the pauses of business, or as they have opportunity, they reflect upon it. This is an excellent plan. It brings the soul into direct contact with God – with His thoughts and His words.

## Spiritual books

We should read good books that have a reviving and spiritual influence upon our minds. A good book is like a good companion: it helps us go on in our heavenly journey. I can never forget the happy influence exerted upon my mind when first I read Baxter's *Saints' Rest*.[14] A good book is a quiet, silent friend. It lies there unobtrusively, waiting patiently until we are ready to take it up, and then it gives us glowing thoughts. Eternity alone can declare the good that has been done by the printing press when consecrated to God. It is impossible to read such books as Jay's *Exercises*, Taylor's *Holy Living*, Owen on *Spiritual-Mindedness*, Cecil's *Remains*, and Nevins' *Practical Thoughts*, without feeling that they draw us nearer to God and heaven.[15]

The memoirs of good people such as Henry Martyn, Edward Payson, David Brainerd, Robert Murray McCheyne, Isabella Graham, Dr. Adoniram Judson, and William Carey are very refreshing to the soul. We catch their spirit to some extent, share with them in their joys and sorrows, and learn to follow them as they followed Christ. While there are many very bad

---

14  Richard Baxter (1615-1691) was an English Puritan pastor and Nonconformist. Some of his writings include *The Reformed Pastor*, *A Call to the Unconverted*, and *The Saints' Everlasting Rest*.

15  *Morning Exercises* by William Jay (1769-1853), *The Rule and Exercises of Holy Living and Dying* by Jeremy Taylor (1613-1667), *Spiritual-Mindedness* by John Owen (1616-1683), *Remains and Miscellanies of the Rev. Richard Cecil* by Richard Cecil (1748-1810), and *Practical Thoughts* by William Nevins (1797-1835).

and foolish books, so bad that they seem as if they had been scooped up out of the pit of perdition, let us thank God that there are books that in tens of thousands of dwellings are speaking for God with a voice that never tires!

## Walk in the Spirit

Do not neglect to pray for the abiding presence of the Holy Spirit. If you are to have solemn, heavenly, elevating thoughts, the Spirit must impart them. If you are to hate sin (Psalm 97:10), pant and thirst after God (Psalm 42:1-2), and long intensely after holiness of heart (Hebrews 12:14; 1 Peter 1:15-16), the Spirit must implant these feelings in your soul. Every glimmer of holy light and every spark of celestial fire that comes into our darkness and coldness comes from this divine Agent. Let it be your earnest, constant prayer that you may have His presence with you always.

In the burning words of Dr. Harris, be urged to this:

> O Christians, is there such a doctrine in our creed as the doctrine of divine influence? Is there such an Agent in the church as the almighty Spirit of God? Is He among us expressly to testify of Christ – to be the great animating spirit of His missionary church? Is it true that His unlimited aid can be obtained by prayer – that we can be baptized with the Holy Ghost and with fire? O you who preach, "Believe the

promise of the Spirit, and be saved!" You who love the Lord, do not keep silent! Send up a loud, long, united, and unsparing entreaty for His promised aid! This is what we need, and this is all we need. Until this is obtained, all the angelic agency of heaven will avail us nothing; when it is obtained, all that agency will be unequal to the celebration of our triumphs.

## A good conscience

The young convert must attempt to cultivate great tenderness of conscience. Paul said, *In view of this, I also do my best to maintain always a blameless conscience both before God and before men* (Acts 24:16). Young converts generally have a tender conscience. It may not be as well enlightened as it should be, but it is sensitive and quick to speak for God. If it is dismissed, though, the whole soul will soon feel the shock. If its voice is frequently stifled and its admonitions neglected, the soul will soon walk in darkness. *In whatever our heart condemns us; for God is greater than our heart and knows all things* (1 John 3:20). It is a dreadful thing to sin so that a man's own conscience becomes his bitterest enemy.

A pastor who was called to see a dying man received from his lips the following account:

"Twenty years ago, I was a member of a

church in W—. Then I was tempted and fell into drinking. I became intoxicated, was called to trial, refused to make a proper acknowledgment of my sin, and I suppose my name was stricken from the church membership book. But God's eye has watched me ever since in all my crooked ways. I see how reluctant He has been to let me go. He has brought me in a way that I knew not, and He has never given me up. Oh, He has been so good, so merciful, so kind, so long-suffering to me!"

"But," said the pastor, "how do you feel when you think how you have treated Him?"

"Oh," he said, in tones of deepest anguish, "that's what hurts me; that's what hurts me."

Yes, the stings of a rebuking conscience are hard to bear, but it is still a more dreadful thing to have a conscience that has ceased to rebuke. A good conscience is one that speaks loud enough to be heard, that speaks truth when it is heard, that speaks in time to prevent the commission of evil, and that perseveres in speaking until it is obeyed.

James Brainerd Taylor[16] says in his journal that it is a bad sign when we find ourselves looking back to past

---

16  James Brainerd Taylor (1801-1829) was an American evangelist.

Christian experiences for evidences of piety. The one who professes Christianity and does not keep a clear conscience is nearly always found doing just that. How much better to keep a sweet, present consciousness of the divine favor, like the man who, when asked if he wished to recover from his sickness or not, said, "Really, my friend, I do not care which. If I die, I will be with God; if I live, God will be with me."

We now speak of some hindrances that lie in the pathway to glory.

## Unequally yoked

Uniting in marriage with one who is not a Christian is a great hindrance. There is no earthly relation so tender, so intimate, as that of a husband and wife. If there is a radical difference of tastes and inclinations between them, if one has an indifference or an aversion to what the other regards of supreme importance, there is a sad drawback upon the happiness of both. Especially when the subject of Christianity, the greatest and most important subject that can engage the human mind, is the subject of difference, there will be a tendency to compromise, and in Christianity, this is always dangerous. We have enough hindrances to encounter from our own hearts, from the world, and from the circumstances in which we are often placed – without deliberately choosing a lifelong hindrance in our bosom companion.

> Uniting in marriage with one who is not a Christian is a great hindrance.

Suppose a devotedly pious young lady is united to a man who is not a Christian. He may not persecute her for living by her biblical convictions, though that is often done, but he will have no sympathy with her in those things that are dearest to her heart. He will look coldly upon her Christian feelings and observances. Perhaps he will even sneer at them. At first, it may be by way of joking, but afterwards it will be in bitter sincerity. To get him to go with her to church, she is tempted to promise to go with him to places that her conscience does not approve, and thus a great wrong is done to her moral nature. There is no family prayer, no spiritual conversation, no cooperation from him in her Christian activities, and no good scriptural hope of spending an eternity with him in heaven. It is easy to see what a sad drawback upon holy progress all this will be. It is true that she may be the means of her husband's conversion, but sadly, it is more often the case that he becomes the cause of her apostasy.

Every pastor is familiar with the gradual steps of spiritual decline. She stops teaching her Sunday school class. She begins missing the prayer meetings. She only attends once on the Lord's Day, and sometimes not even that often. She stops handing out tracts. In short, her connection with other Christians becomes a mere matter of form. When spoken to upon the subject, her excuse is, "You know that my husband is not a sincere Christian, and I cannot follow Jesus as I want to."

When a pious husband is married to an unconverted wife, the influence upon him is equally bad. The power of a woman's influence is a favorite topic with orators, and too much can hardly be said about it, but it is a power for evil as well as for good, depending upon how it is used. A good woman is a crown of glory to her husband and will prove a blessing to him, both for time and eternity; but many a promising young man has been utterly ruined by uniting himself to an unconverted woman, who by her lighthearted, thoughtless, carefree, and extravagant conduct has destroyed his hope for both worlds. *An excellent wife is the crown of her husband, but she who shames him is like rottenness in his bones* (Proverbs 12:4).

> How many people has the attainment of wealth in this life made poor forever!

If they have children, the influence of the mother upon them is disastrous. In short, the result is often that the husband yields point after point to the opposition of his wife until there is little left of his Christianity but the name, if even that remains. We could not expect better from the willful violation of God's rule: *Do not be bound together with unbelievers* (2 Corinthians 6:14), and marry *only in the Lord* (1 Corinthians 7:39).

## Too focused on this life

The last hindrance I would mention is becoming too much engaged in our lawful, worldly business. How many people has the attainment of wealth in this life made poor forever! When David Garrick was showing Dr. Samuel Johnson around his new house and estate and through his splendid parlors, he said, "Ah, David, these are the things that make deathbeds terrible!"

How many professing Christians I have seen make their business their idol, giving their days and nights up to it until it seemed as if they had no concern for anything else! The fruit such people reap is misery.

We are told that a young person once expressed his surprise to Benjamin Franklin that the possession of great riches was so often accompanied by anxiety and unhappiness. The young man referred to the case of a rich merchant who did not seem nearly as happy as some of his own clerks.

Benjamin Franklin took an apple from a fruit basket and gave it to a child in the room who could barely grasp it in his little hand. He then gave the child a second apple, which filled the other hand. Then choosing a third apple of great size and beauty, he presented that to the child also. The child tried to hold the three apples, but failed, and dropping the last one on the floor, burst into tears. "See," said Franklin, "there is a little man in the world with more riches than he can enjoy."

Some time ago two gentlemen stepped into the same compartment of a railway train just as it was starting from Greenwich to London. One of them was a minister of the gospel, and the other man was a rich merchant of high standing in the city. The merchant held a paper in his hand that he was reading with great uneasiness. At last he exclaimed, "Well, that is enough to drive anyone crazy!"

The minister looked at him kindly and said, "I hope, sir, that nothing serious has occurred to disturb you."

"Serious enough, I assure you," was the reply, and he handed him the paper he had been reading. The minister saw that it was a printed list of that day's London stock market prices. Supposing that he had lost money by some quick stock buying-and-selling speculation, he handed the paper back to the merchant, remarking that those who meddled with such matters must expect to suffer losses sometimes.

"Oh," said he, "you are mistaken. I have suffered no loss. The truth is, I purchased some stock some time ago at sixteen dollars a share. I sold it a few days ago for forty-three, but now I saw that I could have gotten forty-six! That's the thing that troubles me so much."

The minister spoke to him affectionately and earnestly about his soul, and upon asking him if he attended any place of worship, he replied, "I go to church as regularly as to the stock exchange, but I can't say that I get much good, for the world rushes on me like a flowing tide, and my mind becomes distracted with thoughts about this and thoughts about that, so that the best sermons are, in a great measure, wasted on me. I have been very successful, but the sad thing is that the more money I make, the more miserable I become. Why, sir, in business, *business* is the heart of my existence. It seems absolutely necessary to my life, and yet, sad to say, it is proving the only misery of it. I am becoming its most burdened laborer and its most absolute slave, and how I am to rid myself of it is more than I can tell."

Poor man! While he poured out his feelings, he became very much affected and wept bitterly.

As my pastoral duties have been mostly in cities, I have seen a great deal of this kind of thing – men killing themselves by inches, body and soul, in the service of the things of this life. Of course, this is done under some pious pretense, such as wanting only to obtain an income, to provide for their own households, and to obtain means to do good. But in almost every case of this extreme devotion to business, it is the love of gain that is the propelling motive. As Henry Ward Beecher has aptly said, "Many men want wealth – not a competence alone, but a five-story competence. Everything subserves this; and religion they would like as a sort of lightning rod to their houses, to ward off, by and by, the bolts of divine wrath."

> A wide heart and a wide estate seldom go together.

This grasping spirit of greed and speculative gain is like the morbid appetite of the drunkard, strengthened and increased by indulgence. All the warm, generous impulses of the soul become repressed and die out. The heart becomes contracted by selfishness. The eyes have nothing looking out of them but greedy planning. Good bargains have far more attractions than good actions.

The noble, generous, benevolent souls around us that are blessing the world with deeds of love are not those who are very rich. A wide heart and a wide estate seldom go together. Indeed, the man who does his duty to his God and to his fellow men can never be very rich. A man can only become very rich either by defrauding others or by defrauding himself. Many people who in their business transactions have been strictly honest to those with whom they did business, have been dishonest to themselves. When these people die, it may be said of them, as Wesley said of someone, "He died wickedly rich."

Seek the true riches – be *rich toward God* (Luke 12:21). Your fields may be fruitful, but your heart barren. Your shop may be prospering, but your soul bankrupt. You may have a hospitable home in which you entertain your friends in a princely style, while you shut the door of your heart in your Savior's face. Lay up treasure in heaven, where funds never depreciate, and where gold never changes its value. *Do not store up for yourselves treasures on earth, where moth and rust destroy, and where thieves break in and steal; But store up for yourselves treasures in heaven, where neither moth nor rust destroys, and where thieves do not break in or steal; for where your treasure is, there your heart will be also* (Matthew 6:19-21).

With your weary, worn, troubled heart, restless as the heaving, moaning sea, cling to Jesus for sweet repose! Weary of the world with its wasting cares, toils, and unsatisfying pleasures, weary of yourself with your broken vows, empty resolutions, and purposeless determinations – cling by faith to Him who has promised to give rest to your soul!

# Chapter 10

# The Spiritual Mind

A spiritual mind enjoys life and peace. It lives as always seeing the invisible God. A carnal mind tends to desire blatant materialism. It seeks to live far away from God. It separates God and His gifts, and even separates God and His works. That is why people of carnal minds, instead of meeting God and holding communion with Him in nature and providence, love to speak of God as having left everything up to fixed and unchangeable laws. They speak as if God were no longer absolute, but that He had become the slave of certain laws that so control all things that it is vain to expect God's personal ministry in our everyday wants and wishes. They thus make prayer a useless thing, and they mock at the idea of a special providence in the affairs of men. Such people would like to exclude God from His own universe, but the Lord reigns, and therefore the righteous rejoice! *The LORD reigns; let the earth rejoice* (Psalm 97:1).

## God is near

The Bible tells us that God's government over the world is precise and personal. God Himself rules, not mere agents and laws. A sparrow falling by the skill of a hunter might seem to be a very chance event, but our Lord tells us that even there the divine direction is at work (Matthew 10:29). God makes use of laws and agents, but He is always through them, in them, and above them by His own personal presence.

This truth lies at the very foundation of all true worship. To feel that God is about my path, and about my bed, and looking upon and taking an interest in all my ways brings Him very near. It leads to an acknowledgment of Him in all that we do. It inspires the soul with a wish to carry all our needs, cares, and troubles to Him as our best Friend. It strengthens our faith and kindles our love into a mighty flame. It enables us to talk with God face-to-face as Moses did of old. We feel that He is at work, not merely among the stars, but also upon our hearts. We believe that He is not only attending to the revolution of mighty worlds, but also to the smallest matter that concerns our well-being. We believe that God is here now, never absent from us for a moment, and He is a very present help in time of trouble. *God is our refuge and strength, a very present help in trouble* (Psalm 46:1).

How noble and glorious is a life lived for God! There are multitudes of such lives. In obscurity and retirement, beneath the shadow of the humblest dwelling, utterly unknown to fame and not caring to be known, they find their all in God. In poverty, in adversity, amid the surging billows of outward troubles – their calm trust in God never wavers. Their hearts beat with a quicker throb at the mention of the name of Jesus, and rather than desert His cause, they would face death in its worst forms. Their warm love for souls is never chilled by the cold atmosphere of selfishness that surrounds them. Despite injury and insult, despite misconception and scorn, they can return good for evil and pray for those who despitefully use them (1 Peter 3:9; Luke 6:28).

## A spiritual mind

Having a spiritual mind is one of the highest proofs of a renewed heart. A person of a poetic mind and of a cultivated taste may take great delight in God's works and yet be far from God Himself. The rush of the mighty waterfall, the lofty overhanging cliff, the sunlit cloud, and the star-filled heavens may thrill him with joy, and yet God may not be in his thoughts. He may utter many sentimental expressions about the greatness and goodness of God, and yet he may love sin as much as ever, and hate holiness as much as ever.

If asked how we can know when the sanctifying grace of God is operating in the heart, we could not point to better evidence than the mind being fixed on heavenly things. *Where your treasure is, there your heart will be also* (Matthew 6:21). God is the treasury of the real Christian, and heaven is the place where

He is most perfectly enjoyed. To have the affections set upon heaven is proof of a truly spiritual mind. The most extensive knowledge, the most profound learning, the most remarkable gifts, an always generous hand, and a tongue always speaking for the cause of Christ may all fail to prove that the heart is right with God; but a heart always soaring heavenward is evidence that none can doubt.

Consider a Christian of little ability, one whose lack of knowledge exposes him to the contempt of the learned, whose intellect may be so weak that he can hardly follow a logical argument to its close, whose stammering tongue refuses to give expression to the warmer emotions of the heart – yet his affections and desires rest in God. He has chosen Him as his portion, and his longing for holiness finds expression in the cry: *Oh, that I had wings like a dove! I would fly away and be at rest* (Psalm 55:6). He looks upon that day as lost in which he has not had a refreshing view of the love of Jesus and of his heavenly home.

What are wealth and fame and all that ambition craves compared to the possession of such a state of mind as this? How refreshing and profitable is the conversation of such a Christian! He comes from communion with God, fragrant with the breath of heaven. He pours out spiritual treasures. His words, his looks, and his tones all tell us that he has been drinking of the river of life and feasting on angels' food.

If a person is thought to be greatly honored who lives in earthly courts and who is in daily conversation with earthly kings, how much more is he honored who is the favorite of the King of Kings! As the greatest mountains are those whose summits reach nearest heaven, so he is the greatest person in God's sight who is found most often soaking his soul in the beams of the Sun of Righteousness.

## True joy

We will be happy just in proportion as we have this spiritual mind. The Bible everywhere speaks of the life of a true Christian as being a happy one. *Joy inexpressible and full of glory* (1 Peter 1:8) and peace *which surpasses all comprehension* (Philippians 4:7) are terms in which it is spoken of.

The early Christians, amid the heaviest trials, had a joy that was the very symbol of heaven itself. They stood steadfastly bearing their testimony for the truth through long years of suffering. Their faith grew stronger and larger until their last hour on earth. Their examples shine down on us through all the thick darkness of intervening ages. This is all because they lived constantly *as seeing him who is unseen* (Hebrews 11:27).

As the most cold and frozen countries are those that are the farthest from the direct rays of the sun, so the reason why we have so many cold professors of the truth now is that they live so far from God.

If we would only collect our thoughts that are often taken up with amusement and entertainment and other empty things of this world, if we would only put the curb of restraint upon our wandering imaginations and bend all our energies to the study of spiritual things, we might (as it were) live in the very suburbs of heaven. David says the light of God's countenance gladdens the heart more than corn and wine (Psalm 4:7), and therefore, he who lives most in the radiance of that countenance will be the happiest.

Many speak as if their lack of peace and joy was their misfortune rather than their sin, but this is a mistake. The gospel is good news, glad tidings for all people. If we are not made happy by it, it is because we have not believed it, and in God's sight, unbelief is a sin worthy of eternal condemnation. God does not communicate joy to the soul without the exercise of its powers any more than He gives us food for our bodies without exercise. If a farmer were to refuse to plow, sow, and work, he would be unreasonable to expect a crop. So it is that joy comes to the soul when we exercise our faith. Lift your thoughts on high! Focus your affections on heaven! The thought of a Savior's love has made thousands welcome the flames of martyrdom and made them joyfully accept the plundering of their possessions that they might obtain an enduring inheritance. It can give you the same blessedness.

> A spiritual mind is the best preservative against temptations to sin.

## A right view of sin

A spiritual mind is the best preservative against temptations to sin. Satan's harvest time is when the Christian's mind is in a carnal, worldly state. Then he employs all his enticements and shoots forth his fiery darts, as it was when David was upon his housetop, idly wasting time and neglecting duty. It was then that the temptation was presented to his mind that produced such terrible results.

Every Christian knows that a heavenly state of mind makes sin appear exceedingly sinful to them. They can then say to every suggestion of the Enemy, *Get behind Me, Satan* (Matthew 16:23). A person employed in mighty affairs upon which life and death depend has no inclination to turn aside to the silly amusements of children. It is the same with those who are absorbed with the momentous concerns of eternity.

Besides, such a person has a deeper view of the evil of sin than others. He has such an overwhelming view of its God-dishonoring nature, such a conception of the emptiness of the world, and such a humbling sight of his own natural depravity that temptations lose their power over him. *It is useless*, says Solomon, *to spread the baited net in the sight of any bird* (Proverbs 1:17), and so it is nearly in vain for Satan to spread his net when the soul sees its danger. This is why Satan is said to darken the mind and to blind the eyes of his victims, and so take them captive at his will. *The god of this world has blinded the minds of the unbelieving so that they might not see the light of the gospel of the glory of Christ, who is the image of God* (2 Corinthians 4:4). *With gentleness correcting those who are in opposition, if perhaps God may grant them repentance leading to the knowledge of the truth, and they may come to their senses and escape from the snare of the devil, having been held captive by him to do his will* (2 Timothy 2:25-26). It is when people have allowed the Enemy thus to blind them that they make such foolish bargains as to prefer their own will to Christ's, sin to holiness, and hell to heaven.

If we spent our time in feeding on the heavenly manna and tasting the delights of heavenly things, sin would be so bitter to our taste that we would turn away from it with unutterable loathing. If Satan had come to tempt Peter to deny his Master when he was on the Mount of Transfiguration, he would have tempted him in vain, but when he found him out of the path of duty in worldly company, he succeeded. The children of Israel in the valley ate, drank, and rose up to dance before their idol; but Moses, who had just come down from conversing with God, had no such desire, but on the contrary, his very soul loathed their unholy proceedings.

So, my reader, if you want to resist the devil so that he will flee from you, set your heart and desires on things above. *Submit therefore to God. Resist the devil and he will flee from you* (James 4:7). *Therefore if you have been raised up with Christ, keep seeking the things above, where Christ is, seated at the right hand of God. Set your mind on the things above, not on the things that are on earth* (Colossians 3:1-2).

## Hot for Christ

The cultivation of a spiritual mind gives new life and vigor to every duty. It is high time that Christians become very ashamed of their coldheartedness in

## THE SPIRITUAL MIND

Christ's service. They profess to believe the most sublime truths, and yet they often talk of them with frozen lips and cold hearts. They profess to pray and sing the praises of God, but they do so with an apathy that dwindles down into heartless forms.

How are we to get out of this cold and heartless state? What will give new power to our prayers and make our songs like those of the angels above? I answer: cultivating a mind that lives in God's own immediate presence. Heavenly-minded Christians are lively and joyful Christians. It is only when we look at heavenly things from a great distance and through the thick clouds of worldly-mindedness that we become dull and dead; but when we live in the presence of the living God, what a power and dignity there is about us! If such a man be a minister, how heavenly and spiritual are his sermons!

> What will give new power to our prayers and make our songs like those of the angels above?

If a person is a simple member of the body of Christ, his prayers, his conversation, and his exhortations are like the distant echoes of the transporting strains that fill the courts of heaven. After a person has set his affection on heaven, he soon begins to emit so many of heaven's rays that people say, "Surely that person has been with God on the holy mount."

For lack of such heavenly-mindedness, many who profess to be Christians are like lamps that are not lit, and their duties are like sacrifices without fire. But when we get a live coal from off the heavenly altar (Isaiah 6:6), how freely do our sacrifices burn! When we light our lamps at the flame of God's love, they shed a brilliant radiance all around.

Let us lift our hearts to heavenly things! Let us gaze with the eye of faith upon the living Savior, beholding His beauty, glory, and excellency, and soon the fire of divine love will consume the dross in our hearts, and the fire thus kindled will not be strange fire (Leviticus 10:1)! Zeal brought about in this way will be lasting zeal. While some, like Baal's priests, will be ready to cut themselves because their sacrifices will not burn, the truly spiritually-minded man will ascend in a chariot of devotion to heaven (1 Kings 18:28; 2 Kings 2:11). Such a Christian is profitable to all around him. He is as salt to the earth, a light in the midst of surrounding darkness (Matthew 5:13-16).

While the worldly man will talk of nothing but the world, the scholar will talk of his learning, and the self-righteous person will talk of his good deeds, the spiritually-minded person talks of the things that are eternal. His words pierce, melt, and often transform the heart of those who hear them. His conversation is like the box of precious ointment that the woman poured upon the head of Christ (Matthew 26:7). It fills the whole house with a heavenly aroma.

If you go to that person's house and sit at his table, your soul will find a feast of heavenly manna. Travel with him by the way, and he will try to direct and inspire you on your journey to heaven. He will try to make you rich in faith and an heir of eternal glory. If you wrong such a person, he can forgive you as he himself has been forgiven. If others curse him, he prays for blessings on them. This is the man of the right quality, and the world is better off because of him. Like Caleb and Joshua, he has gone to the heavenly country and has brought in a bunch of the heavenly fruit to whet our appetite for more (Numbers 13). *How blessed are the people whose God is the LORD* (Psalm 144:15).

## Comfort and peace

A spiritual mind is the best support amid the sorrows and the afflictions of life. Many different methods are adopted for meeting those trials to which all are subjected. Some people struggle under them and render themselves and all those around them miserable by pouring forth their ineffective complaints. Others sit down with a fatalistic indifference, submitting to the beatings of something they call fate. Others, leaning upon a false philosophy, try to find comfort for themselves in the utterance of the poor excuse that since we can't help it, we must just submit. Of all such comforts it may be said, as of Job's friends, *Sorry comforters are you all* (Job 16:2).

When trouble comes to the spiritually-minded person, he has a far better means of comfort. When distress and sufferings rob him of all outward comfort, Jesus comes into his soul and says, *Peace be with you* (John 20:21). When Paul and Silas were thrust into the inner prison, their bodies scarred by scourges and their feet made fast in the stocks, their unfettered souls soared to heaven in a song of praise. No one could put a lock and key upon their affections. In the same way, the martyrs have often enjoyed that peace in the midst of the flames that their persecutors could not find on a bed of feathers.

Thus it was that Abraham went out, not knowing where he was going, but *looking for the city which has foundations, whose architect and builder is God* (Hebrews 11:8-10). This is why Moses esteemed the *reproach of Christ greater riches than the treasures of Egypt; for he was looking to the reward* (Hebrews 11:26). This is why others were *tortured, not accepting their release, so that they might obtain a better resurrection* (Hebrews 11:35).

> When we think for a moment of the glorious privileges that belong to the Christian, not a murmuring word should ever proceed from our lips.

When we think for a moment of the glorious privileges that belong to the Christian, not a murmuring word should ever proceed from our lips. Why would we not be happy and content when we are every moment under the special care of that loving Father for whose power nothing is too vast and for whose inspection nothing is too minute? We are enabled by the eye of faith to look full on His brightness and to commune with Him face to face. The treasures of God's precious promises pour their untold riches into our souls and afford us an unperishable source of delight.

Why would you not be happy if your name is recorded in the Lamb's Book of Life (Revelation 21:27), your future home is a house not made with hands (2 Corinthians 5:1), and a crown of glory awaits your coming (1 Peter

5:4)? The Christian's Savior has ransomed him by His obedience *to the point of death, even death on a cross* (Philippians 2:8), and declared his salvation a finished work. It is evident that a person who lives and walks under the influence of such truths as these has comfort in affliction and a balm for sorrow that others cannot possibly possess.

What does it matter even if a whole shower of afflictions may fall upon the Christian, like the stones upon the head of Stephen, if, like him, he can see, from the opening heavens, the sympathizing eye of his Savior fixed upon him! *But being full of the Holy Spirit, he gazed intently into heaven and saw the glory of God, and Jesus standing at the right hand of God; and he said, Behold, I see the heavens opened up and the Son of Man standing at the right hand of God* (Acts 7:55-56).

So what if the Christian is doomed to solitude, like John in Patmos, if, like him, he can hear the voice of his Lord speaking comfort and cheer! What does it matter if he is put into the fiery furnace of affliction, like the three Hebrews, if, as with them, the Son of God walks with him in the fiery trial (Daniel 3:25)! What if, though, like Paul, he may have a thorn in the flesh, but, like him, he can hear his Lord say, *My grace is sufficient for you* (2 Corinthians 12:7-9)! What if, though, like Peter, Satan may desire to have him that he might sift him as wheat, but, like him, he has the Lord's assurance, that *I have prayed for you, that your faith may not fail* (Luke 22:31-32)!

## Chapter 11

# Hindrances and Helps to Spiritual-Mindedness

If you want to possess a spiritual mind, you must avoid living in the indulgence of any known sin. Sin is the cause of all the misery that exists in our world. It wrings the heart with anguish from the cradle to the grave and makes every part of our world echo the groans of suffering humanity. It has introduced death and has made a huge sepulcher of our world. It is still emptying earth and populating perdition. It is our only enemy, for it does that for us which nothing else can: it makes us hideous in the sight of God.

### Oppose sin

A person can be extremely poor on earth and yet be the favorite of God. Like Lazarus and Job, he may be covered with a loathsome disease and yet be fair and lovely in God's sight. Sin is the abominable thing that the Lord hates. It is more poisonous than the venom of asps, though people often cherish it as a sweet morsel under their tongues.

People might think lightly of sin and call it just a little thing, but can that be a little thing that causes the God of love to curse the work of His own hands and to banish those from His presence forever for whom He has done so much?

If this is the nature of sin, there can be no heavenly delights in the heart where sin is willingly indulged. If a person is daily ignoring his conscience and sinning against the clearest light, if he is in a great measure the slave of his appetite and passions and refuses to restrain them, if he is in a hurry to be rich and does not care at all about the means by which this is to be attained, and basically, if he does not seek to cultivate a conscience that retreats from the least approach of iniquity, then thick clouds of darkness will come between him and God. When he attempts to soar heavenward, he will be like a weak bird that would try to follow the lofty flight of the eagle, but which the wind beats back panting and nearly lifeless to the earth. A person who does not hate sin may try to stir up his mind in emotion and blow upon his little spark of love, hoping to kindle a flame, but his sin, like water poured upon a flame, will quickly put it out.

Count Gondomar (1567-1626), when near the eternal world, said that he feared nothing in the world more than sin, and that whatever liberties he had formerly taken, he would rather now submit to be torn to pieces by wild beasts than knowingly or willingly commit any sin against God.

The last words of Archbishop James Ussher (1581-1656) were, "Lord, forgive my sins, especially my sins of omission."

If a professed Christian would rather gossip at home than go to a prayer meeting, if he would rather go to hear fifty sermons than live out one, if he finds it more pleasant to criticize his minister than to pray for his success – then he cannot be heavenly-minded. If he would rather talk about a thousand sins in his neighbors than overcome one in himself, if he can back away from any Christian duty because it is unpopular and might bring upon him the world's ridicule, if he acts as if he thought that Christ was holy in order to allow him to be unholy, then he does not have a heavenly mind.

He might seem to pray with the earnestness of an Elijah, talk with the feeling of a David, and weep like a Jeremiah, but if he does not strive against sin as those men did, and act out his convictions of right as they were accustomed to do, there is much reason to fear that he is only deceiving himself. Indulging in sin will clip the wings of the strongest faith and cut the sinews of the warmest zeal. God's people are to be *a people for His own possession, zealous for good deeds* (Titus 2:14).

## Avoid covetousness

If we want to develop a spiritual mind, we must shun all covetousness. The Word of God is most direct on this point, assuring us that where the love of the world is, the love of the Father cannot dwell. *Do not love the world nor the things in the world. If anyone loves the world, the love of the Father is not in him* (1 John 2:15).

When the worldly-minded man should be rejoicing in God, he is rejoicing in the increase of his earthly riches instead. When he should be mourning over the low spiritual condition of the church and over perishing souls, he is weeping over his earthly losses. If such a one like this who professes to follow Jesus could see his conduct in the light of a burning world and in the light of eternity, he would be startled at the extent of his own foolishness!

How great is the foolishness of those who rush into innumerable cares in their eagerness to be rich, and after they have involved themselves in more than they can possibly manage, they wonder that they do not make more progress heavenward! You might as well call upon a rock or a mountain to fly heavenward as to expect that your soul can hold daily communion with God while it groans under such a load.

The curse of God seems to have rested upon covetousness from the beginning of time, and no wonder. What keeps the hungry from being fed? What keeps the naked from being clothed and the ignorant from being instructed? What keeps the Word of God from being known over the whole earth and the world from being evangelized? There is only one answer: covetousness. It is a barefaced refusal to do what God wants to be done with His own. It is usurping God's right, which is a sin as bad as usurping His throne.

It was this sin that ruined the first pair of humans, for they coveted to be as gods. Covetousness found lodging in the heart of Cain, who coveted Abel's blessing (Genesis 4:4-5). It was the sin that ruined Lot's family, transforming his wife into a pillar of salt (Genesis 19:26). It caused Achan to be stoned to death (Joshua 7:20-21) and made Gehazi leprous until his death (2 Kings 5:20-27). It brought ruin on Judas (Matthew 26:15), death on Ananias (Acts 5:1-5), and caused Demas to forsake the truth (2 Timothy 4:10). In short, it was this sin that can be said to have made hell itself, for hell was made for devils who coveted the throne of God.

Rev. Richard Cecil had a rich hearer, who, when a young man, had asked his advice. Mr. Cecil had not heard from the rich, young man in a while, so he visited him one day. He said, "I understand you are very dangerously situated."

The young man replied, "I am not aware of it."

Mr. Cecil said, "I thought you might not be aware of it, and therefore I have called on you. I hear you are getting rich. Take care, for it is the road by which the devil leads thousands to destruction."

Charles Finney tells about a merchant in one of the towns in the state of New York who was paying a large part of his minister's salary. One of the members of the church was telling this fact to a minister from abroad, speaking of the sacrifice that this merchant was making. At this moment the merchant came in.

"Brother," said the minister, "you are a merchant. I suppose you employ a clerk to sell goods, and you pay a schoolmaster to teach your children. You tell your clerk to pay the schoolmaster out of the store's profits a certain amount for his services in teaching. Now suppose that your clerk would tell people that he had to pay the schoolmaster's salary, and he told of the sacrifices he was making to do it. What would you say to this?"

"Why," said the merchant, "I would say it was ridiculous."

"Well," said the minister, "God employs you to sell goods as His clerk, and He employs your minister to teach your children. He requires you to pay his salary out of the income of the shop. How do you call this *your* sacrifice and say that *you* are making a great sacrifice to pay this minister's salary? No; you are just as much bound to sell for God as he is to preach for God. You have no more right to sell goods for the purpose of laying up money than he has to preach the gospel for the same purpose. You are bound to be just as holy and to just as much desire the glory of God in selling goods as he is in preaching the gospel. You are just as absolutely to give up all your time to the service of God as he does.

"You and your family may live out of the profits of this store, and so may the minister and his family, just as lawfully. If you sell goods from these motives, selling goods is just as much serving God as preaching, and a man who sells goods upon these principles and acts in conformity to them is just as pious, just as much in the service of God, as he is who preaches the gospel. Everyone is bound to serve God in his calling – the minister by teaching, the merchant by selling goods,

## Seek humility

If we want to be spiritually minded, we must avoid a proud and lofty spirit. There is no disposition that seems more out of place in anyone than pride and self-conceit, yet how generally are these character traits exhibited! Remembering that man is a fallen creature, depraved and guilty, that he has derived his origin from the dust and is fast hastening to the grave, where worms will devour him, what has he to be proud of? He is dependent upon God every moment for every pulse that beats, every breath he draws, and everything that makes life desirable.

> If we want to be spiritually minded, we must avoid a proud and lofty spirit.

He is even dependent upon the smallest and most despised of God's creatures for many of his comforts, and even necessities. Everything that he calls his own he holds with the most slippery grip. His friends might be snatched from him in a moment, his riches may make themselves wings and fly away, and his health may be blasted by disease in any passing breeze. He is susceptible to hunger and thirst, cold and heat, poverty and disgrace, and sorrow and pain through all the brief span of his stay upon earth. Even his mind – his noble, intellectual part, that part that can rise to heaven and wander through eternity – is liable to be taken from him at any moment, leaving him a babbling fool.

It is said that the celebrated poet Robert Southey (1774-1843) for some years before his death had so lost his intellectual powers that he did not know his own name, and when looking at his own books said, "Southey! Who is he?"

Tourney, after he had excelled all Oxford in learning and had become very eminent among the literary men of Paris, was so puffed up with pride as to claim that Aristotle was superior to Moses and Jesus Christ, and yet only equal to himself. In his latter days he became so mindless as not to know one letter in a book or to remember one thing he had ever learned.

Yet poor mortals will dare to be proud! Some glory in their wealth, some in empty titles, some in beauty and high birth, and others in empty fame. Oh, pride must certainly stand as a mighty foe between God and the soul!

A young lady in New York City, eighteen years of age, was brought up by her parents in all the fun and vanity of youth. She was encouraged by them to dress in the fashion of the world and to take part in all the frivolities and entertainment she could. When she was suddenly taken ill, three physicians were immediately sent for, and they pronounced her to be close to death.

No sooner was their opinion made known to her than she requested, as a favor, that all her fun companions might quickly be brought to see her. They were soon around her bed, and she told them she was going to die. She described the awful manner in which they had spent their precious time, and in a very affecting manner she exhorted them all to repent before it was too late. Then, turning to her father and mother, she said to them, in the presence of her acquaintances, these heartrending words: "You have been the unhappy instruments of my being; you encouraged me in pride and led me in the paths of sin. You never once warned me of my danger, and now it is too late! In a few hours you will have to cover me with dirt; but remember, while you are casting the dirt upon my body, my soul will be in hell – and you are the cause of my anguish!"

Soon after, she died.

If you want to enjoy real communion with God, you must beware of pride. If pride drove the first pair from an earthly paradise, rest assured that if you indulge pride, it will drive you from a heavenly paradise. We are told that God knows the proud afar off (Psalm 138:6). If you are puffed up in your own conceit, greatly delighted when people praise you, and correspondingly depressed when they disapprove; if you love best the company of those who flatter you, and avoid those friends who are ready to tell you your faults; if you are ready to take offense on account of some imaginary disrespect or insult, and refuse to confess your own faults when you do wrong; if you hate plain speaking, but are always ready to assert your own greatness – then it is to be feared that there is much pride hiding in your heart.

As long as someone worships himself, he cannot worship God. He may make use of very humble expressions and describe himself as a great sinner, but this might only be the proud spirit seeking applause for its seeming humility.

## Spiritual conversation

If we want to enjoy spiritual-mindedness, we must often be occupied in conversation about heavenly things. There is a great deal of religious conversation, as it is called, that is little better than religious gossip. What is called religious conversation often consists only of talking about ministers and their sermons, missionaries and their labors, and churches and their rituals.

It is good for a person to be well-informed in regard to what is happening in the Christian world, but it is not right if our conversation is only about the mere externals of religion, to the exclusion of those vital themes that cause the heart to burn and glow, as we speak of them. The two disciples, in that delightful walk that they had with Jesus after His resurrection, said, *Were not our hearts burning within us while He was speaking to us on the road, while He was explaining the Scriptures to us?* (Luke 24:32).

John Bunyan was converted by overhearing the conversation of two humble women talking about the love of Christ to them.[17] Christians who neglect to speak of divine things lose many precious opportunities of usefulness.

Some years ago, a Christian minister who was returning from preaching in a neighboring village was asked by an individual to direct him to a certain place. His request was attended to, and when the stranger was thanking him for his kindness, the minister replied,

---

[17] You can read about Bunyan's conversion in *Grace Abounding to the Chief of Sinners*, available from ANEKO Press.

"Take care, my friend, that you are in the right way at last."

These words kept ringing in the man's ears, and he wondered what the minister meant by them. He thought about them often, and those words in time led to the salvation of his soul. Some years went by, with all their accompanying cares, joys, and sorrows, when the minister was asked to preach in another town. After the service, he was requested to visit a member of the church who was dying. As soon as the minister came near, the dying man fixed his eyes on the minister, and with a peculiarly significant look and emphatic voice said, "Sir, I know you! I know you!"

"Know me!" replied the minister. "How can that be? I am a stranger here."

"I know you, sir," he replied. "Do you not remember, some years ago, a person asking you the way to such a place, and you returned with him, led him in the right path, and when you were parting, you said to him, 'Take care, my friend, that you are in the right way at last'?"

"No, I do not," replied the minister, for it had completely escaped his memory.

"Well, you did, sir," the dying man replied. "I have not forgotten it, nor will I ever forget it. 'The right way at last!' Oh, sir, am I in that way now? I will not live long. I feel that I am dying. Tell me, please tell me, if I am in the right way!"

The minister questioned him as to his faith in Christ and on other important points, to which the dying man returned suitable and satisfactory answers. The minister then affectionately and earnestly recommended him in prayer to God and left him. In a few days, the man's mortal career was ended.

## Prayer and song

Nothing promotes spiritual-mindedness as much as conversing with God in prayer and praise. In everything we are invited to make our requests known unto Him and to mingle thanksgiving with our supplications. *In everything by prayer and supplication with thanksgiving let your requests be made known to God* (Philippians 4:6). Singing the praises of God is to be a large part of what we do in heaven.

Very persistent efforts have been made in the present day to discourage people from prayer, on scientific principles, but this is just another form of the old opposition of the carnal heart to communion with God. The natural heart hates anything that brings a personal God near it. Still, every Christian knows, from the best of all evidences – his own experience – that God is the Hearer of prayer. The world is full of evidences of it, no matter how sinners may shut their eyes and close their ears against them. Let us not cease to call upon God while He is near and to acknowledge Him in everything so that He may direct our steps. *Seek the LORD while He may be found; Call upon Him while He is near* (Isaiah 55:6). *Trust in the LORD with all your heart and do not lean on your own understanding. In all your ways acknowledge Him, and He will make your paths straight* (Proverbs 3:5-6).

# Chapter 12

# Consecration

On a beautiful summer day, you may have seen the clouds curtain the heavens with darkness until all nature seemed to shudder under the threat of a coming tempest. You may have then seen the thundercloud torn in two by the blazing thunderbolt and the teeming shower discharged. The clouds then passed away, and the sky became lovelier and the atmosphere more balmy and pleasant than before.

So it is with the soul to whom God's salvation from sin has come. God says to him, *I have wiped out your transgressions like a thick cloud* (Isaiah 44:22), and there is joy and sunshine in his soul. The dark cloud of sin has rolled away from his mind, and the love of the infinite Father falls upon his soul with celestial light. He can look up to heaven, down to hell, and all around him in the world, and give utterance to the bold challenge: *Who is the one who condemns? Christ Jesus is He who died* (Romans 8:34).

The gospel does not merely save from the punishment of sin – from hell and eternal woe – but it also saves from the power of sin. It does this to people of all classes and nations. It takes hold of the very worst; none are too bad, none have sunk too low, none have wandered too far, but this salvation can reach and save them. It takes hold of the heart of the very vilest, and it never leaves him until he is rejoicing in glory and striking the strings of the golden harp to the praise of his blessed Redeemer!

Yet our Lord has told us that our life on earth is to be marked by struggle and trial. We are told that it is through much tribulation that we must enter the kingdom (Acts 14:22). There was no keeping hidden the trials of a holy life. Jesus told His disciples that they could expect a steady opposition and hostility to their Christianity and their attempts to do good. They did not fully realize this, and they must have been greatly astonished when the storm of the world's scorn, indignation, and malignity burst upon their heads.

> Our Lord has told us that our life on earth is to be marked by struggle and trial.

We live in a time when the danger is greater to our souls than in the days of fiery persecution. When a form of religion is in a manner popular, when attendance upon public worship gives a certain respectability to people, and when gain can be made of godliness, then allurement of a worldly kind proves itself more dangerous to eternal interests than direct persecution. Persecution, with its loud blasphemies and its hands red with blood, brought out the graces of God's Spirit in a race of glorious martyrs who stood steadfast and immoveable for their principles, and the gospel came out of the conflict triumphant. *Therefore, my beloved brethren, be steadfast, immovable, always abounding in the work of the Lord, knowing that your toil is not in vain in the Lord* (1 Corinthians 15:58).

Now, however, the world comes with its polite and smooth speech, speaking favorably of many of the outward things of religion, but ridiculing all that constitutes its vital power. Many become weak in their Christian lives, cast aside a desire to be holy, throw themselves upon the trends and fashion and direction of culture, and make shipwreck of their souls!

We need more of the firmness of the old Puritan who, when told that he was too stern and precise about some things in his Christian walk, said, "Sir, I serve a precise God." It was said of a righteous man that he sometimes seemed to make little things great, but that he never made great things little.

We now need consecration to God, as much or even more than those who lived in the stormy ages. By consecration to Christ, I do not mean a new conversion, as some have called it, nor a state of sinless perfection, as others have claimed. It is not a thing of sudden impulses and emotions developed in a moment of excitement. It is simply the soul trusting wholly in Jesus, washed from all its sins in His precious blood, and clinging with an undying grasp to His cross. It is giving yourselves up to Christ forever, as bought with a price, and feeling that you are no longer your own.

If there was ever someone entirely consecrated to God, it was the apostle Paul, and he expressed it in the words, *But may it never be that I would boast, except in the cross of our Lord Jesus Christ, through which the world has been crucified to me, and I to the world* (Galatians 6:14), and *I determined to know nothing among you except Jesus Christ, and Him crucified* (1 Corinthians 2:2). Paul expressed it in that wonderful prayer when he asked that we might be *filled up to all the fullness of God* (Ephesians 3:19). We get this only in Christ, for *in Him all the fullness of Deity dwells in bodily form* (Colossians 2:9).

## Only in Christ

To try to build up a consecration to Christ by resolutions and promises of our own is like trying to build up a wall of sand that runs down as fast as you stack it up, or like trying to carry water in a leaking pitcher. An old writer says, "Wisdom out of Christ is damning folly; righteousness out of Christ is guilt and condemnation; sanctification out of Christ is filth and sin; redemption out of Christ is bondage and slavery."[18]

The person consecrated to God has given up his will in order to be governed by God's will. He seeks to be of one mind with God. He does not measure himself or his works by the world's standard, but by what the Lord has spoken. In order to be of a strong, steady purpose to glorify God by doing those things

---

18  This quote is from Irish pastor Robert Traill (1793-1847), quoted in J. C. Ryle's tract, "We Must Be Holy."

that are pleasing in His sight, a consecrated Christian seeks to make the Lord Jesus his bright pattern and example in all things. He desires to have the same tender love for souls that Jesus had, the same forgiving spirit to enemies, the same boldness and consistency in defending the right, the same willingness to help the suffering and the oppressed, and the same prayerfulness and love for communion with heaven. Basically, as an old writer says, a consecrated Christian desires to be "a little Christ."

This was the one great aim and purpose for which Christ came into the world. *He died for all, so that they who live might no longer live for themselves, but for Him who died and rose again on their behalf* (2 Corinthians 5:15). He gave Himself for us that He might redeem us from all iniquity and make us *a people for His own possession, zealous for good deeds* (Titus 2:14). He tells us that if we love Him, we will keep His commandments (John 14:15).

A holy life is the only evidence that we have a living and not a dead faith. It is an evidence of the reality of true Christianity that the world cannot deny. A holy life is a preparation for heaven, for heaven is a place where nothing unholy can enter. Indeed, if it were possible for an unholy person to enter there, it would be no heaven to him. He would not be able to enjoy it. One reason that the true Christian longs to get to heaven is that he will be sinless there.

I read a beautiful illustration of this. It is as follows:

> If a child had been born and spent all his

life in the Mammoth Cave, how impossible would it be for him to comprehend the upper world! His parents might tell him of its life, and light, and beauty, and its sounds of joy; they might heap the sand into mounds, and try to show him by pointing to stalactites how grass, and flowers, and trees grow out of the ground, till at length, with laborious thinking, the child would fancy he had gained a true idea of the unknown land. And yet, though he longed to behold it, when the day came that he was to go forth, it would be with regret for the familiar crystals, and rock-hewn rooms, and the quiet that reigned therein. But when he came up, some May morning, with ten thousand birds singing in the trees, and the heavens bright, and blue, and full of sunlight, and the wind blowing softly through the young leaves, all a-glitter with dew, and the landscape stretching away green and beautiful to the horizon, with what rapture would he gaze about him, and see how poor were all the fancyings and the interpretations which were made within the cave, of the things which grew and lived without; and how he would wonder that he could have regretted to leave the silence and dreary darkness of his old abode! So, when we emerge from this cave of earth into that land where spring growths are, and where is summer, and not that miserable travesty which we call summer here, how shall we wonder that we could have clung so fondly to this dark and barren life![19]

True happiness on earth is only to be found in God's favor, and that favor is only to be found at the cross. Christ is to us the manifested God. *No one has seen God at any time; the only begotten God who is in the bosom of the Father, He has explained Him* (John 1:18). Christ is the means by which the great fountain of God's love is made accessible to us so that we can drink and live.

> True happiness on earth is only to be found in God's favor, and that favor is only to be found at the cross.

We are so made that we are restless and uneasy and dissatisfied until we find peace with God, and it is for us as free as the air we breathe! We are a burden to ourselves, we are our own tormentors, until we come to Him to get rest. When we come to Calvary, God reveals His loving presence to us, and the still, small voice whispers of love. There we find a hiding place – not from justice, for justice was fully satisfied – but from our own guilty fears. There the soul finds God as its portion forever, and no other portion can satisfy! *My flesh and my heart may fail, but God is the strength of my heart and my portion forever* (Psalm 73:26).

People desire to be part of the world, but their groans

---

[19] From *Life Thoughts, Gathered from the Extemporaneous Discourses of Henry Ward Beecher* by Edna Dean Proctor (1858).

of disappointment come back to our ears on every breeze. They seek satisfaction in money, friends, fame, in titles, in a constant whirl of games and amusements, and in many sinful pleasures; but from them all comes the cry of dissatisfaction. While they are devising new ways of finding pleasure, the great reaper, Death, comes and cuts them away.

When we turn to God, through Christ, He is ever ready to pardon our sins, to show compassion for our weakness, to strengthen our powers, and to glorify our immortal nature with the fullness of His love. We can turn from all our sin, frailty, and trouble, from our broken vows and baffled resolutions, to the strength of the eternal God. *Trust in the LORD forever, for in GOD the LORD, we have an everlasting Rock* (Isaiah 26:4). Nearer and nearer to Him as the great center of blessedness, let your soul mount up on wings as eagles (Isaiah 40:31).

## Fully for God

Let your consecration to God be wholehearted and complete. Let the solemn words of the Bible draw and bind you. You are not your own. You are bought with a price. You were not redeemed with corruptible things, such as silver and gold, but with the blood of the Son of God (1 Corinthians 6:19-20; 1 Peter 1:18-19). It is then dishonest to feel that anything we have is our own, and to be devoted to selfish purposes. What do we have that we have not received (1 Corinthians 4:7), and that, too, for the purpose of glorifying God? The noblest use to which anything can be put is in the service of the Giver of every good and perfect gift. *Every good thing given and every perfect gift is from above, coming down from the Father of lights, with whom there is no variation or shifting shadow* (James 1:17).

Our bodies are not our own. This is the lowest part of our nature – the part that sprang from the earth and goes back to it again. It is the habitation of the soul, during our earthly time here, and the agent by which the soul puts forth the efforts to do good. We are fearfully and wonderfully made, and the organization of our bodies shows forth the wisdom of our Creator in such a manner as to fill the thoughtful mind with awe. *I will give thanks to You, for I am fearfully and wonderfully made; Wonderful are Your works, and my soul knows it very well* (Psalm 139:14).

However, we are to use our bodily powers for God. If we have physical strength, it should be used for His glory. It is not something to be proud of, but is something to be thankful for and to be used for useful works and to help bear the infirmities of the weak. Our blessed Lord had a body like ours, subject to the same infirmities. His body tended to get tired like ours does, His heart was subject to being distressed, and His feelings were able to feel reproach as ours are – yet it was in that body that He did good and went about continually doing good.

Let our feet be used on errands of mercy and our hands in works of benevolence. Our eyes are to seek out the needy and the perishing, and our ears ought to hear the cry of the distressed and drink in the promises of God. We are to be careful of our health so that we can work longer and better for Christ. The strength derived from our food is to be given back to God in honest work, such as will be well-pleasing in His sight. The body is not to be made an instrument of mere selfish indulgence, but is a means by which we should glorify God and benefit our fellow men on earth.

Our souls are not our own. God breathed into man and he *became a living being* (Genesis 2:7). That soul has the stamp of God's immortality upon it. It must live as long as He lives. When the sun will have shot forth its last ray and all the hosts of the stars will have been quenched in darkness, the soul will still live in immortal youth.

The possession of such a wonderful gift makes us jump back with fright at ourselves. As has been said, if we were assured that the butterfly that flutters in the summer breeze, or the bird that sings on the tree, had begun a life that could never end, with what interest we would look at them. In the same way, we know that every child we see and every human being we meet can never die, but must live somewhere, in some condition, forever!

Christ, who came from His throne at the very summit of glory to save souls, who wept over them when He saw them rushing on to ruin, and who died to save them, knew the worth of such a soul as no one else could know. He says, *For what will it profit a man if he gains the whole world and forfeits his soul? Or what will a man give in exchange for his soul?* (Matthew 16:26). That soul, with its vast powers and capacities, its wonderful range of understanding, its capability of enjoying or suffering – for that soul to be lost is a greater calamity than it would be for the whole material universe to be swept out of existence!

We have been given such a soul, but it is not our own in the sense that we can do what we please with it and go unpunished. We have no right to destroy such a soul. Every provision has been made for its purification and perfection in bliss. The Spirit of God offers to come and dwell in it and guide it to heights of attainment, both here and hereafter, which we now are not able to comprehend.

> Let all our powers, without reserve, be dedicated to God's service.

Let all our powers, then, without reserve, be dedicated to God's service. Let our memories be stored with His thoughts and words. Let reason, judgment, conscience, imagination, emotions, and feelings all be consecrated to Him who laid down His life for us. This is but a reasonable service, and to keep anything back is to rob God. *Present your bodies a living and holy sacrifice, acceptable to God, which is your spiritual service of worship* (Romans 12:1).

## Use all for God

It is truly sad to think how many noble intellects have been misused for the worst purposes. People of noble talents who might have written with the wisdom of a John Milton have instead written works indulging sin. To put ridicule into the mouths of drunkards against Christianity and virtue, to stimulate the depravity of youth, to promote the bad habits and ways of sinful adults, to wrap the elegance of eloquence and the charms of genius around deadly errors that lead people down to destruction – this is the bad distinction which they have attained. What a fearful account must such people render to the Judge of the whole earth!

Our time is not our own. Time is very closely allied to eternity. Every hour of time is laying up results for heaven or hell. Time lost can never be recalled. All the regrets, tears, and prayers of all the ages could not bring back to us one misspent day. Yet people often speak of time as a burden hanging upon their hands, and they exercise great ingenuity to devise means, as they say, "to kill time."

If we could have spent only one day with the Lord Jesus when He was upon earth and could have seen how He spent His time, what a rebuke it would have been to how we spent our time! He went about continually doing good from morning till night. He was always at His work of love, and His motto was, *We must work the works of Him who sent Me as long as it is day* (John 9:4). Even as a child, He was always about His Father's business (Luke 2:49).

Time is a sacred responsibility to be accounted for, and should be used, not for our own personal gratification, but for the honor of the Great Master. Time used for God is happy time. It leaves no sting behind in the memory, but is pleasant to reflect upon on a deathbed.

Our money is not our own. As proof that God does not regard the money a person has as his own, He often takes it away from him in His providence, and leaves him in poverty. Money is needed to spread the gospel, to circulate the Bible, to feed the hungry, and to nourish the sick. To accomplish these things, money must be consecrated to God by those who are consecrated to Him. We have no right to draw upon the funds of God to supply our lusts and pride, but only our necessities. Real good for time and eternity can be done with it now. The cause of truth and humanity is in difficulty for need of it.

In the great day of account, what will all the wealth in the world seem in comparison to the salvation of one single soul? "I have nothing to spare," is often the plea of a shameful reluctance, but a very different calculation will be found in the light of a burning world. Then those who, by acts of self-denial, have sought to bless the world, will hear the Judge say, *Whatever you did for one of the least of these brothers and sisters of mine, you did for me* (Matthew 25:40).

I do not need to mention this further. The principle is plain. We have nothing that we can really call our own – nothing but our sins! The gifts that God has given us were imparted to us not to promote self-indulgence, but for the common good of the world. The great truth that we have been bought with the blood of Jesus leaves us under lasting obligation to spend and to be spent – in His service.

## Chapter 13

# How to Make a Success of the Christian Life

There are two types of people who start out in the Christian life: those who make a complete or partial failure of it, and those who make a complete success of it. The question at once suggests itself, Is it possible to point out a plain pathway in which anyone who wants to succeed in the Christian life can walk, and following that pathway will make success absolutely sure? I believe it is. God's Word gives a few simple instructions which, if followed, will make success in the Christian life a certainty.

There are seven steps in the path marked out in the Bible.

### 1. Begin Right

We see in John 1:12 what a right beginning is: *But as*

*many as received Him, to them He gave the right to become children of God, even to those who believe in His name.* Receive Christ.

Take Him as your Savior. He is the one who died for your sin. Trust the whole matter of your forgiveness to Him. Rest upon the fact that He has paid the full penalty of your sin. *He made Him who knew no sin to be sin on our behalf, so that we might become the righteousness of God in Him* (2 Corinthians 5:21). *Christ redeemed us from the curse of the Law, having become a curse for us - for it is written, Cursed is everyone who hangs on a tree* (Galatians 3:13).

It is in this first step that many people make a mistake. They try to mix in their good works as a ground of salvation. They think that God will forgive them if they are good, because of Christ's death *and* their goodness.

Take Him as your Deliverer. He is the one who will save you from the power of sin and will give you life when you are dead in trespasses and sins. Don't try to save yourself from the power of sin. Trust Him to do it.

Take Him as your Master. Don't seek to guide your own life. Surrender unconditionally to His lordship over you. Say, "All for Jesus!" Many people fail because they back away from this entire surrender. They want to serve Jesus with half their heart, part of themselves, and part of their possessions. This life of halfhearted surrender is a miserable life of stumbling and failure. The life of entire surrender is a joyous life all along the way.

If you have never done so before and want to make a success of the Christian life, get alone with God, get down on your knees, and say, "All for Jesus!" Say it very earnestly. Say it from the bottom of your heart. Stay there until you realize what it means and what you are doing. It is a wondrous step forward when one really takes it. If you have taken it already, take it again. Take it often. It always has fresh meaning and brings fresh blessedness.

> Taking Christ as your Master involves obedience to His will.

Taking Christ as your Master involves obedience to His will, as far as you know it, in even the smallest detail of life. This is one of the most essential conditions of receiving *the Holy Spirit, whom God has given to those who obey Him* (Acts 5:32).

## 2. Confess Christ Openly before Others

*Therefore everyone who confesses Me before men, I will also confess him before My Father who is in heaven* (Matthew 10:32). *For with the heart a person believes, resulting in righteousness, and with the mouth he confesses, resulting in salvation* (Romans 10:10).

The life of confession is the life of full salvation. It is when we confess Christ before others that He confesses us before His Father in heaven, and it is then that the fullness of His blessing comes. It does not mean that we are to confess Jesus just once, but constantly. The one who desires to make the most success of the Christian life should seize every opportunity to confess Christ Jesus before others – in the home, at the store, at work, in the church – everywhere.

I once heard a wise, old preacher say, "If we make a good deal of Christ, He will make a great deal of us." How many backsliders fell away from Christ at this point! They went to a new city or a new place to work, and they neglected to confess Christ – and now they are back in the world.

## 3. Study the Word

*Like newborn babies, long for the pure milk of the word, so that by it you may grow in respect to salvation* (1 Peter 2:2). The Word of God is the soul's food. It is the nourishment of the new life. Anyone who neglects the Word cannot make much of a success of the Christian life. All who progress in the Christian life spend much time reading the Word of God.

Many people fail here. Ask any backslider, "Have you fed on the Word daily?" I have never found one backsliding person who could say that he had.

Here are two points on Bible reading: first, read for food for your own soul; second, read a great deal on your knees. The Bible has become in some measure a new book to me since I started reading it on my knees.

## 4. Pray without Ceasing

*Pray without ceasing* (1 Thessalonians 5:17). The person who would succeed in the Christian life must lead a life of prayer. This is easy enough if you determine to do so. Have set times for prayer. The rule of David and Daniel, praying three times a day, is a good rule.

*Evening and morning and at noon, I will complain and murmur, and He will hear my voice* (Psalm 55:17). *Now when Daniel knew that the document was signed, he entered his house (now in his roof chamber he had windows open toward Jerusalem ); and he continued kneeling on his knees three times a day, praying and giving thanks before his God, as he had been doing previously* (Daniel 6:10).

Begin the day with thanksgiving and prayer – thanksgiving for the specific mercies of the past, and prayer for the specific needs of the present day. Stop in the midst of the bustle and worry and temptation of the day and take time for thanksgiving and prayer. Close the day with thanksgiving and prayer.

There should also be special prayer in times of special temptation – when we see the temptation approaching. Keep looking to God. *Pray without ceasing.* It is not needful to be on our knees all the time, but the *heart* should be on its knees all the time. If "Satan trembles when he sees the weakest saint upon his knees,"[20] let us keep him trembling all the time. We should be often on our knees and on our faces, literally. This is a joyous life, free from worry and care. Neglect of prayer is where many fail.

There are three things for which the one who is determined to make a success of the Christian life must especially pray:

1. Wisdom. *If any of you lacks wisdom, let him ask of God* (James 1:5).

---

[20] This is from the poem/hymn, "What Various Hindrances We Meet," by William Cowper (1731-1800).

2. Strength. *Those who wait for the LORD will gain new strength* (Isaiah 40:31).

3. The Holy Spirit. *If you then, being evil, know how to give good gifts to your children, how much more will your heavenly Father give the Holy Spirit to those who ask Him?* (Luke 11:13).

If you have not yet received the baptism with the Holy Spirit, you should offer specific prayer for this specific blessing, and specifically expect to receive it. If you have already received the baptism with the Holy Spirit, you should pray to God for a new filling with the Holy Spirit with each new emergency of Christian work.

## 5. Go to Work for Christ

*For to everyone who has, more shall be given, and he will have an abundance; but from the one who does not have, even what he does have shall be taken away* (Matthew 25:29). Note the context, and you will see that this means that those who use what they have will get more, and those that let what they have lie idle will lose even that. The working Christian, the one who uses his talents, whether few or many, in Christ's service, is the one who makes progress in the Christian life here, and who will hereafter hear, *Well done, good and faithful slave. You were faithful with a few things, I will put you in charge of many things; enter into the joy of your master* (Matthew 25:23).

Find some work to do for Christ and do it. Seek for

work. If it is nothing more than distributing tracts or Christian books, do it. Always be looking for something more to do *for* Christ, and you will always be receiving something more *from* Christ.

## 6. Give Generously

*The generous man will be prosperous* (Proverbs 11:25). *He who sows sparingly will also reap sparingly, and he who sows bountifully will also reap bountifully. Each one must do just as he has purposed in his heart, not grudgingly or under compulsion, for God loves a cheerful giver. And God is able to make all grace abound to you, so that always having all sufficiency in everything, you may have an abundance for every good deed* (2 Corinthians 9:6-8).

> A stingy Christian cannot be a growing Christian.

Success and growth in the Christian life depend on few things more than upon generous giving. A stingy Christian cannot be a growing Christian. It is wonderful how a Christian begins to grow when he begins to give.

Give systematically. Set aside for Christ a fixed portion of all the money or goods you get. Be exact and honest about it. Don't use it for yourself under any circumstances. A tenth is a good portion to begin with. Don't let it be less than that. After you have given your tenth, you will soon probably learn the joy of giving freewill offerings in addition to the tenth.

## 7. Keep Pushing On

*Brethren, I do not regard myself as having laid hold of it yet; but one thing I do: forgetting what lies behind and reaching forward to what lies ahead, I press on toward the goal for the prize of the upward call of God in Christ Jesus* (Philippians 3:13-14). Forget that which lies behind; press on to the better things that lie ahead.

Forget the sins that lie behind. If you fail anywhere, if you fall, don't be discouraged. Don't give up. Don't agonize over the sin. Confess it instantly. Believe God's Word: *If we confess our sins, He is faithful and righteous to forgive us our sins and to cleanse us from all unrighteousness* (1 John 1:9). Believe that the sin is forgiven. Forget it and press on.

Satan misleads many poor souls here. He keeps us agonizing over our failures and sins. He even makes us think this is humility, as if it were humility to doubt God's Word and make Him a liar by not believing that the sin is forgiven and put away when He says it is.

Forget the achievements and victories of the past, and press on to greater achievements and victories. Satan tries to cheat us out of the greater life. He keeps us thinking so much about what we have already obtained and makes us so contented with it and so puffed up over it, that we come to a standstill or even backslide.

I have seen this in many individuals and many churches. "How well we have done!" they think. Our only safety is in forgetting those things that are behind, and pressing on. "Excelsior! Higher!" should be the soul's persistent cry. Press on! There is always something better ahead. You may have received a second blessing, or a twenty-second, but there is still something better until we *attain to the unity of the faith, and of the knowledge of the Son of God, to a mature man, to the measure of the stature which belongs to the fullness of Christ* (Ephesians 4:13).

Young Christian friends and older Christians – the road to certain success in the Christian life is plain enough. Will you take it? The truths of this chapter are familiar, but are you practicing them? Read this chapter again often, and see if there is some point at which you fail. If you find that there is, correct your mistake at once.

## Appendix A

# How to Use the Bible

1. Own a good-print, well-bound Bible, a concordance, and a topical Bible.[21]

2. Set a portion of each day sacredly apart for Bible study. Let your body go unfed rather than your immortal soul. (Acts 17:11)

3. Choose an hour for study when your mind is clearest.

4. Study with a humble, teachable mind, not to see what you can make the Scriptures teach, but what God meant it to teach. (Matthew 11:25)

5. Pray for the guidance of the Author of the book. (Psalm 119:18; John 14:26; 1 John 2:27)

6. Read the whole Bible through consecutively from beginning to end, again and again. (Luke 24:27)

---

21 Today there are many computer software programs that contain many commentaries, topical Bibles, concordances, multiple Bible versions, maps, and much more. One recommended example is e-Sword (e-sword.net), which contains many of these basic features for free.

7. Study rather than skim. Weigh each word. Look up all references and read them carefully. Search the Scriptures with the topical Bible and concordance to see how God handles such words and subjects as *sin*, *salvation*, *cross*, *blood*, *repentance*, *faith*, etc. Analyze books of the Bible verse by verse, writing down what you have learned from each verse. (Joshua 1:8)

8. Read it as it is – as the *Word of God* (1 Thessalonians 2:13). Submit your judgment unhesitatingly to its teachings, believe *all* its promises, heed *all* its warnings, and obey *all* its commands, always and immediately. Remember, it is God's message to you.

9. Study and accept not only what you like, but all that God has to say. (John 7:17)

10. Commit to memory at least one verse each day. (Psalm 119:11)

11. Carry a Bible or New Testament with you so you can make good use of spare time. (Ephesians 5:16; Acts 8:28)

## Appendix B

# Tips for True Christian Living

*To Be Frequently Read and Constantly Followed*

1. All promptings of duty are leadings of the Spirit. Follow them always and at any cost. (Ephesians 4:30; 1 Thessalonians 5:19)

2. Never go where you cannot take Christ with you. (Matthew 28:20; Psalm 139:7)

3. Never go where you would not be glad to have Christ find you if He would come. Never do what you would not be glad to have Christ find you doing. (Matthew 24:44-51; Luke 21:34-35; 1 Thessalonians 5:2-4)

4. Do not do anything that you are not confident you can do to the glory of God. (Colossians 3:17; 1 Corinthians 10:31)

5. When in doubt as to any proposed action, do not do it if it is clear that loyalty to Christ does not positively demand it. (Romans 14:22-23; 1 John 3:21)

6. Seek the blessing of God upon all that you do. (Psalm 127:1; Philippians 4:6-7)

7. Do not try to see how little Christ will accept from you, but try to see how much you can do for Him. (2 Corinthians 5:14-15; 1 Chronicles 4:10)

8. The best person is an unsafe example, so follow Jesus only. (Jeremiah 17:5; Galatians 2:11-13; John 8:12)

9. Seek at once and continually an enduement of power from on high. (Luke 24:49; Acts 2:39; 4:31)

10. Take all your doubts, troubles, and burdens to Jesus, and leave them with Him. (Matthew 11:28-29; Psalm 55:22; Isaiah 50:10; 1 Peter 5:7)

11. Trust your salvation wholly to God. (Ephesians 2:8; 2 Corinthians 2:9-11; 1 Peter 1:5; Jude v. 24)

# Robert Boyd – A Brief Biography

Robert Boyd was born on August 24, 1816, in Girvan, South Ayrshire, Scotland. Robert grew up learning the ways of God. He learned to pray every morning and evening. He memorized the entire book of Psalms and other entire chapters of the Bible. He also spent much time reading good Christian books, *The Pilgrim's Progress* being one of them.

When Robert was about twelve years old, his family moved to Glasgow. Robert's spiritual life began to suffer, as he made some friends who led his heart away from God. God was looking out for Robert, though, and brought him back to Himself. When Robert was about fifteen years old, he went to hear a preacher who was plain and direct and full of Christ, and it was then that Robert gave his heart and life to Jesus. He left his ungodly friends and got more involved in Christian activities.

Robert became sick for a while, but used the time to read many Christian books by men such as Ralph Erskine, Thomas Boston, John Flavel, Richard Baxter, and John Bunyan. Robert Boyd began to prepare himself for what he believed God had for his life's work – to be a minister of the gospel. However, when Robert's father suddenly died, Robert had to give up his studies and find work. He was employed to go around and speak on behalf of the growing temperance movement, encouraging people to abstain from alcohol.

He also began doing missionary work in the city. He began giving talks during the week and preaching on Sundays, where his preaching resulted in spiritual awakening. Robert joined a Baptist church in Stirling, where he soon became the new pastor after the former pastor suddenly died. Robert wanted to proclaim Christ Jesus in every sermon. "I did not like to preach a single sermon without explaining how a sinner can be saved," he said. Robert Boyd was determined to live his life fully for God and to always be in close communion with Him.

On April 6, 1840, Robert Boyd married Christina Forbes. Robert and Christina had nine daughters, one of whom died in infancy in Scotland. Boyd continued his pastoral and temperance work in Stirling, as well as undertaking evangelistic work in and around Edinburgh. His health began to suffer, and he tried to find strength and rest by visiting the seashore, but his health did not improve. He made the difficult decision to go to North America.

Upon arriving in Montreal, Canada, on September

25, 1843, Boyd began preaching. He became the pastor of a new Baptist church in Brockville, Ontario. After pastoring there for seven years, Boyd spent five years pastoring a church in London, Ontario, before accepting a call to a Baptist church in Hamilton, Ontario. However, his poor health still troubled him. His father-in-law had recently died and had left them his small farm, so the Boyds soon moved to the farm in Waterville, Wisconsin, where he rested for about ten months, obeying the doctor's orders.

Boyd then traveled ten miles back and forth every weekend to preach at a Baptist church in Waukesha, Wisconsin, but soon moved his family to Waukesha where he could more fully carry out his pastoral duties. In 1856, Boyd visited some friends in Chicago, taking time to preach there too. Some who heard him preach had been considering starting a church in the southern part of the city, and they thought Boyd was the right man for the job. So in September 1856, the Boyds moved to Chicago.

Boyd's communion with God and desire for the lost led to many conversions and times of revival wherever he preached. As he began pastoring in Chicago, there was so much interest in spiritual things that Boyd held meetings every night for months, and people met to pray every morning. There were also meetings at noon, and Boyd spent the afternoons visiting people to discuss their souls. He speaks of this time as the happiest time of his life.

However, his health again suffered. He spent a few months near Cleveland seeking rest and healing. Upon his return to Chicago, he resumed his labors, and in 1862, the congregation moved to a larger building on the corner of Wabash Avenue and 18th Street. Boyd continued what pastoral duties he could, and he also ministered to Confederate prisoners.

Boyd often had to preach while sitting down, and even had to be carried in to preach at times. He soon resigned from his pastoral position. During his twenty-seven years as a pastor, he had preached more than eleven thousand sermons, in addition to giving other talks and lectures. He had also officiated at about six hundred funerals, five hundred weddings, and had personally baptized 869 converts.

Robert Boyd then moved back to Waukesha, where his health soon improved so much that he agreed to preach once a week at the Baptist church there. Due to some paralysis in his legs, he still had to be carried in and out and still preached from a chair, but he was glad to have the opportunity to preach once again. Boyd preached in the morning one day in September 1867, and then traveled to Pewaukee to preach in the afternoon, where he would preach his last sermon. He caught a severe cold on the way home, and the inflammation of his spine that he had struggled with for many years led to the partial paralysis that confined him to bed for the rest of his life.

Due to his inability to continue the physical labor of pastoral duties, Boyd began writing articles for a couple Christian publications, which led to him writing books, especially for children and new converts. Boyd found joy and hope in his writings, often receiving letters from people who had been changed by God after reading one of his books.

Robert Boyd's books were simple and plain and were used by God. D. L. Moody distributed thousands of copies of Boyd's *Glad Tidings* at his meetings in Great Britain, saying that he did not know of any better book for those seeking God. Charles Spurgeon recommended Boyd's book, *The World's Hope*. In addition to those two books, Boyd also authored *The Lives and Labors of Moody and Sankey, None but Christ Or the Sinner's Only Hope, Young Converts, Good News*, and others.

Despite Boyd's physical difficulties and his twelve years of being confined to bed and not being able to preach, he said, "God has given me such views of His character and gospel that I cannot be gloomy, much less despairing. Why should a living man complain, and especially a man in whom Christ lives by His Spirit, and to whom He says, *Because I live, ye shall live also*?"

Robert Boyd died at the end of August 1879, but his words live on.

# Other Similar Titles

**ANEKO**
PRESS

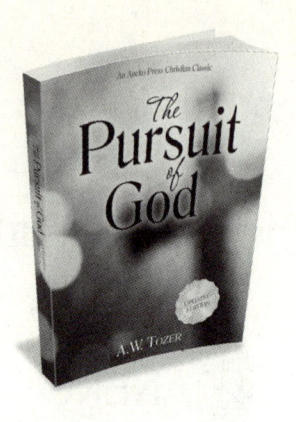

*The Pursuit of God,*
by A. W. Tozer

To have found God and still to pursue Him is a paradox of love, scorned indeed by the too-easily-satisfied religious person, but justified in happy experience by the children of the burning heart. Come near to the holy men and women of the past and you will soon feel the heat of their desire after God. Let A. W. Tozer's pursuit of God spur you also into a genuine hunger and thirst to truly know God.

*Available where books are sold.*

*Pilgrim's Progress,*
by John Bunyan

Often disguised as something that would help him, evil accompanies Christian on his journey to the Celestial City. As you walk with him, you'll begin to identify today's many religious pitfalls. These are presented by men such as Pliable, who turns back at the Slough of Despond; and Ignorance, who believes he's a true follower of Christ when he's really only trusting in himself. Each character represented in this allegory is intentionally and profoundly accurate in its depiction of what we see all around us, and unfortunately, what we too often see in ourselves. But while Christian is injured and nearly killed, he eventually prevails to the end. So can you.

*Available where books are sold.*

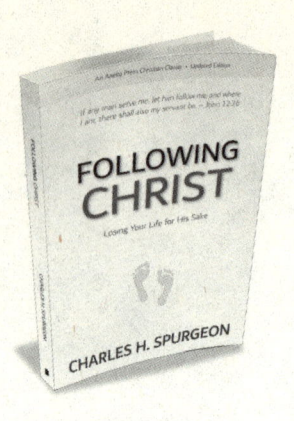

## *Following Christ,*
## by Charles H. Spurgeon

You cannot have Christ if you will not serve Him. If you take Christ, you must take Him in all His qualities. You must not simply take Him as a Friend, but you must also take Him as your Master. If you are to become His disciple, you must also become His servant. God-forbid that anyone fights against that truth. It is certainly one of our greatest delights on earth to serve our Lord, and this is to be our joyful vocation even in heaven itself: His servants shall serve Him: and they shall see His face (Revelation 22:3-4).

*Available where books are sold.*

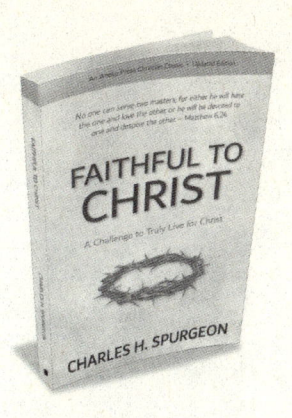

## *Faithful to Christ,*
## by Charles H. Spurgeon

I believe that many Christians get into a lot of trouble by not being honest in their convictions. For instance, if a person goes into a workshop, or a soldier into a barracks, and if he does not fly his flag from the beginning, it will be very difficult for him to run it up afterwards. But if he immediately and boldly lets them know, "I am a Christian, and there are certain things that I cannot do to please you, and certain other things that I cannot help doing even though they might displease you" – when that is clearly understood, after a while the peculiarity of the thing will be gone, and the person will be let alone.

– Charles H. Spurgeon

*Available where books are sold.*

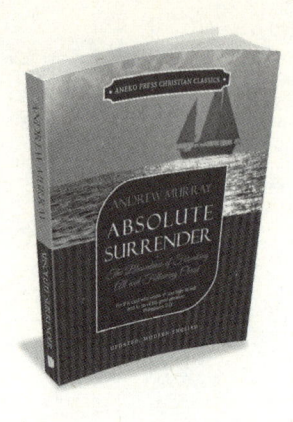

*Absolute Surrender,*
by Andrew Murray

God waits to bless us in a way beyond what we expect. *From the beginning, ear has not heard, neither has the eye seen, what God has prepared for those who wait for Him* (Isaiah 64:4). God has prepared unheard of things, things you never can think of, blessings much more wonderful than you can imagine and mightier than you can conceive. They are divine blessings. Oh, come at once and say, "I give myself absolutely to God, to His will, to do only what God wants." God will enable you to carry out the surrender necessary, if you come to Him with a sincere heart.

*Available where books are sold.*

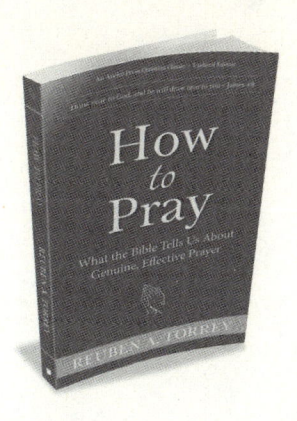

*How to Pray,* by Reuben A. Torrey

Prayer. Satan laughs as he looks at the church today and says to himself, "You can have your Sunday schools and your young people's small groups, your boys' and girls' programs, your vacation Bible schools, your Christian schools, your elegant churches, your retreats, your music programs, your brilliant preachers, and even your revival efforts – as long as you don't bring the power of almighty God into them by earnest, persistent, believing, mighty prayer."

It is not necessary that the whole church prays to begin with. Great revivals always begin first in the hearts of a few men and women whom God arouses by His Spirit to believe in Him as a living God, as a God who answers prayer, and upon whose heart He lays a burden from which no rest can be found except in persistent crying unto God.

*Available where books are sold.*

## *The Overcoming Life,*
## by Dwight L. Moody

Are you an overcomer? Or, are you plagued by little sins that easily beset you? Even worse, are you failing in your Christian walk, but refuse to admit and address it? No Christian can afford to dismiss the call to be an overcomer. The earthly cost is minor; the eternal reward is beyond measure.

Dwight L. Moody is a master at unearthing what ails us. He uses stories and humor to bring to light the essential principles of successful Christian living. Each aspect of overcoming is looked at from a practical and understandable angle. The solution Moody presents for our problems is not religion, rules, or other outward corrections. Instead, he takes us to the heart of the matter and prescribes biblical, God-given remedies for every Christian's life.

*Available where books are sold.*

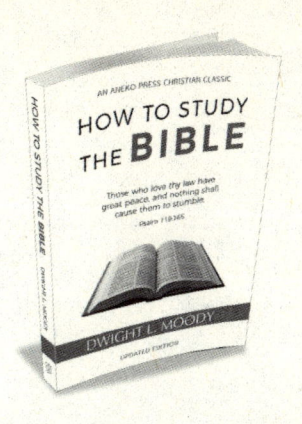

*How to Study the Bible,*
by Dwight L. Moody

There is no situation in life for which you cannot find some word of consolation in Scripture. If you are in affliction, if you are in adversity and trial, there is a promise for you. In joy and sorrow, in health and in sickness, in poverty and in riches, in every condition of life, God has a promise stored up in His Word for you.

*Available where books are sold.*